# Ninja Foodi Smart XL Grill Cookbook 2021

1000-Days Amazing Recipes for Beginners and Advanced Users

(Indoor Grilling & Air Frying Perfection)

Katrina Sowell

# Table of Contents

# Introduction

Have you ever wanted to make one of your favorite grilled foods, but because of some limitations, you couldn't? These days, you can find an indoor electronic grill like the Ninja Foodi Smart XL grill that serves the same purpose as a traditional outdoor grill, and even better. By every standard, I think that this is a worthwhile addition to your collection of kitchen appliances. The device truly lives up to the meaning of its name — Foodi. Aside from basically offering users the option of grilling with creativity, I also discovered that it comes with five other fantastic cooking styles.

## What is Ninja Foodi Smart XL Grill?

With the Ninja Foodi Smart XL grill, you can bake, air fry, roast, broil, or dehydrate your favorite meals. This is also in addition to allowing you to cook healthy meals. It contains the following advantages and features:

• Ninja Foodi Smart XL Grill with Smart Cook System. The Smart XL grill that sears, sizzles, and crisps. Indoor countertop Grill and Air Fryer. Perfectly cook food on the inside to your desired doneness and char grill every side with 500F Cyclonic Grilling Technology and the

Smart Cook System. 500F cyclonic air and the 500F grill grate combine to give you delicious char-grilled marks and flavors

- Smart Cook System—4 smart protein settings, 9 customizable doneness levels, and the Foodi Smart Thermometer enable you to achieve the perfect doneness from rare to well done at the touch of a button. No more guesswork and no more under or over cooking

- XL Capacity—grill 50% more food than the original Ninja Foodi Grill for delicious family sized meals. Grill grate fits up to 6 steaks, up to 24 hot dogs, mains and sides at the same time, and more

- 6 in 1 indoor grill—Grill your favorite foods to char grilled perfection, or go beyond grilling with 5 additional cooking functions: Air Crisp, Bake, Roast, Broil, and Dehydrate

- Air fry crisps with up to 75% less fat than deep frying (tested against hand cut, deep fried French fries), using the included 4 quart crisper basket. Unique Smoke Control System—the combination of our chef recommended grilling practices, a temperature controlled grill grate, splatter shield, and cool air zone reduces smoke, keeping it out of the kitchen

- Forgot to defrost dinner? Transform foods from frozen to perfectly char grilled in under 25 minutes. Dual Sensor Foodi Smart Thermometer—continuously monitors temperature in two places for even more accurate results. Multi task with peace of mind as food cooks to perfection

- Includes: 1760 Watt Ninja Foodi Smart XL Grill, 9" x 12" High Density Grill Grate, 4 Quart Crisper Basket, 6 Quart Cooking Pot, Foodi Smart Thermometer, Cleaning Brush, Chef Created 15 Recipe Book

## The Functions of Ninja Foodi Smart XL Grill

The Ninja Foodi Smart XL grill is packed with 6 protein setting smart cook systems designed to meet almost every grilling need, plus more. Users can choose between beef, poultry, fish, and pork settings. This ensures you get the desired or typical outdoor grill flavor for each meal. It also comes with multiple levels of customizations are perfect match for the doneness your desire in each recipe. In addition to this, you may use any of the 6 cooking functions depending on your choice.

1. **Grilling.** You may check the grilling cheat sheet that comes with your unit to guide you with the time and temperature settings. It is best to check the food regularly depending on the doneness you prefer and to avoid overcooking. Once the required settings are selected, press start and wait for the digital display to show 'add food'. The unit will start to preheat similar to an oven and will show the progress through the display. This step takes about 8 minutes. If you need to check the food or flip it, the timer will pause and resume once the lid is closed. The screen will show 'Done' once the timer and cooking have been completed. Power off the unit and unplug the device. Leave the hood open to let the unit cool faster.

2. **Baking**: this option is perfect for cooking, casseroles, and of course, cakes. However, the fan speed used for this function is slightly lower than that for roasting and air crisping.

3. **Air Crisping**: The air crisping or air frying function allows you to crisp foods with air circulation as against the usual method of frying with oil. Everyone loves the crunchy, crispy feel of fried foods, but not everyone likes the oily part. The air frying function of the Ninja Foodi Smart XL grill offers a great way to make healthy fried foods without the extra days and calories. You may also use it for reheating your foods.

4. **Dehydrate**: this function is equally perfect for reducing the moisture content of your foods. Pet owners may use this function to make treats for their pets. It may require slower fan speed and lower temperatures, but it still produces excellent flavor.

5. **Roasting**: the roasting feature on the Foodi Grill is just perfect for the browning effect you will want on your meats and veggies. The interior of the food gets well cooked, leaving the exterior browned enough without overcooking it.

6. **Broiling**: If you want extra browning on your recipes, you can use the broil function to achieve that.

## Tips to using Ninja Foodi Smart XL Grill

1.   Always prioritize safety and set aside time for reading the user manual that comes along with the Ninja Foodie Smart XL Grill first.

2.   Electric grills may not look like it, but they usually get hot during and after use. Practice caution and use safety tools such as tongs and oven mitts when handling the device and the food.

3.   Place the grill on a heat-proof surface, leaving at least 5 inches of space on all sides for sufficient airflow. Also, do not place it near water to avoid electric shocks.

4.   Allow the device to preheat for a few minutes before adding the food. Preheating will allow the grill to reach the right temperature that will give you evenly cooked and beautifully char-grilled results. Preheating also avoids extended cooking time and food from sticking to the grate.

5.   Lightly grease the grill and basket even though they have nonstick coatings. Steer away, however, from aerosol cooking sprays as these can damage the device. We recommend getting a regular kitchen spray bottle filled with your choice of oil

6.   Overcrowding food tends to obscure the hot air circulation inside, thereby affecting the crispiness and doneness of the food. Larger meats like pork chops, chicken cutlets, steaks, burgers, and fish fillets should be arranged in a single layer and not stacked one on top of the other. Shaking the basket from time to time will also help to make sure everything inside the basket will cook and brown evenly. Use the Foodi Smart Thermometer to check the

doneness of meat accurately. Doing so not only helps to prevent overcooking but also ensures that the food is cooked enough and safe to eat.

7. To get the best results, it's recommended to flip half-way between cooking. This ensures your food cooks very well, and you get those adorable grill marks on both sides.

8. Although the inbuilt technology is designed to ensure efficient cooking without smoking, you may experience smoking in your Foodi Grill from time to time. When this happens, it's typically because air mixes with oils and fats from the previous cookings. In order to prevent smoking, you may use oils with a high smoke point like grapeseed or avocado while grilling.

9. A Ninja Foodi grill is a well-designed appliance, where the parts are removable and dishwasher safe. The shield can go into the dishwasher and can be cleaned easily. At the top of the lid lies a splatter shield that needed to be popped out after every cooking and needed to be cleaned as well. The interior and exterior of the appliance did not get dirty very easily and can be clean regularly with wipe cleaner.

All right. Now that you know about your Ninja Foodi Smart XL Grill, it's about time you dived into the recipes and started grilling!

# Chapter 1: Amazing Breakfast

## Early Morning Burrito

(Prep time: 5-10 minutes; Cook time:30 minutes; For 4 servings)

**Ingredients:**

- 10 whole eggs, beaten
- 12 tortillas
- 1 pound breakfast sausage
- 2 cups potatoes, diced
- 3 cups cheddar cheese, shredded
- 1 teaspoon olive oil
- Salt and pepper to taste

**Preparation:**

1. Pour olive oil into a pan over medium heat
2. Cook potatoes and sausage for 7 to 10 minutes
3. Stir it frequently
4. Spread this mixture on the bottom of the Ninja Foodi Smart XL Grill
5. Season with salt and pepper
6. Pour the eggs and cheese on top
7. Preheat your Ninja Foodi Smart XL Grill by pressing the "BAKE" mode at 325 degrees F temperature
8. Set the timer for 20 minutes
9. Cook for 20 minutes
10. Top the tortilla with the cooked mixture and roll
11. Sprinkle cheese on the top side
12. Add Air Fryer basket to Ninja Foodi Smart XL Grill
13. Air Fry the Burritos for 10 minutes at 375 degrees F
14. Serve and enjoy!

**Nutritional Values Per Serving:**

Calories: 400; Fat: 20 g; Saturated Fat: 10 g; Carbohydrates: 36 g; Fiber: 5 g; Sodium: 675 mg; Protein: 22 g

# Awesome Tater Tots Eggs

(Prep time: 5-10 minutes; Cook time: 25 minutes; For 4 servings)

**Ingredients:**

- 1 pound frozen tater tots
- 1 cup cheddar cheese, shredded
- 2 sausages, cooked and sliced
- Cooking spray as needed
- Salt and pepper to taste
- ¼ cup milk
- 5 whole eggs

**Preparation:**

1. Preheat your Ninja Foodi Smart XL in Bake mode at 390 degrees F for 3 minutes
2. Take a bowl and add eggs, milk, season with salt and pepper
3. Take a small baking pan and grease with oil
4. Add egg mix to the pan and transfer to your Foodi
5. Cook for 5 minutes, place sausages on top of eggs, sprinkle cheese on top
6. Bake for 20 minutes more
7. Serve and enjoy!

**Nutritional Values Per Serving:**

Calories: 187; Fat: 8 g; Saturated Fat: 3 g; Carbohydrates: 21 g; Fiber: 1 g; Sodium: 338 mg; Protein: 9 g

# Awesome Seasoned Broccoli

(Prep time: 10 minutes; Cook time: 10 minutes; For 4 servings)

**Ingredients:**

- 1 pound broccoli, cut into florets
- 1 tablespoon chickpea flour
- ¼ teaspoon turmeric powder
- ½ teaspoon red chili powder
- ¼ teaspoon spice mix
- 2 tablespoons yogurt

- ½ teaspoon salt

**Preparation:**

1. Take your florets and wash them

2. Add all the listed ingredients except florets into a bowl

3. Add broccoli and combine the mix well

4. Keep it aside for 30 minutes

5. Preheat your Ninja Foodi Smart XL Grill by pressing the "BAKE" mode at 400 degrees F temperature

6. Set the timer to 10 minutes

7. Let it preheat until you hear a beep

8. Crisp for 10 minutes

9. Serve and enjoy!

**Nutritional Values Per Serving:**

Calories: 111; Fat: 2 g; Saturated Fat: 1 g; Carbohydrates: 12 g; Fiber: 1 g; Sodium: 024 mg; Protein: 7 g

# Awesome French Burrito

(Prep time: 10 minutes; Cook time: 5 minutes; For 2 servings)

**Ingredients:**

- 2 tortillas
- 2 whole eggs, scrambled
- ½ cup bacon, cooked crisp and crumbled
- ½ cup cheddar cheese, shredded

**Preparation:**

1. Add eggs, bacon, and cheese into a bowl

2. Top the tortillas with the mix

3. Roll the tortillas

4. Transfer it to your Ninja Foodi Smart XL

5. Preheat your Ninja Foodi Smart XL Grill by pressing the "AIR CRISP" mode at 250 degrees F

6. Serve and enjoy!

**Nutritional Values Per Serving:**

Calories: 531; Fat: 15 g; Saturated Fat: 7 g; Carbohydrates: 81 g; Fiber: 2 g; Sodium: 1125 mg; Protein: 18 g

# Hearty Bacon Omelet

(Prep time: 5-10 minutes; Cook time: 10 minutes; For 4 servings)

## Ingredients:

- 4 whole eggs, whisked
- 4 tomatoes, cubed
- 1 tablespoon olive oil
- 1 tablespoon cheddar, grated
- 1 tablespoon parsley, chopped
- ¼ pound cubed, cooked, and chopped
- Salt and pepper, to taste

## Preparation:

1. Add bacon into a small-sized pan
2. Heat the pan over medium heat
3. Sauté for 2 minutes
4. Add bacon with remaining ingredients into a bowl
5. Stir well and sprinkle cheese on top
6. Preheat your Ninja Foodi Smart XL Grill by pressing the "BAKE" mode at 400 degrees F temperature
7. Set the timer to 10 minutes
8. Pour the mixture into a baking dish
9. Transfer it to your Ninja Foodi Smart XL Grill
10. Bake for 8 minutes
11. Serve and enjoy!

## Nutritional Values Per Serving:

Calories: 311; Fat: 16 g; Saturated Fat: 4 g; Carbohydrates: 23 g; Fiber: 4 g; Sodium: 149 mg; Protein: 22 g

# Crispy Mac and Cheese

(Prep time: 5-10 minutes; Cook time: 10 minutes; For 4 servings)

**Ingredients:**

- 1 tablespoon parmesan cheese, grated
- Salt and pepper to taste
- 1 and ½ cheddar cheese, grated
- ½ cup warmed milk
- ½ cup broccoli
- 1 cup elbow macaroni

**Preparation:**

1. Preheat Ninja Foodi Smart XL by pressing the "AIR CRISP" option and setting it to "400 Degrees F" and timer to 10 minutes
2. let it preheat until you hear a beep
3. Take a pot and add water, allow it to boil
4. Add macaroni and veggies and broil for about 10 minutes until the mixture is Al Dente
5. Drain the pasta and vegetables
6. Toss the pasta and veggies with cheese
7. Season with some pepper and salt and transfer the mixture to your Foodi
8. Sprinkle some more parmesan on top and cook for about 15 minutes.
9. Allow it to cool for about 10 minutes once done
10. Enjoy!

**Nutritional Values Per Serving:**

Calories: 180; Fat: 11 g; Saturated Fat: 3 g; Carbohydrates: 14 g; Fiber: 3 g; Sodium: 287 mg; Protein: 6 g

# Peanut Butter and Banana Chips

(Prep time: 5-10 minutes; Cook time: 15 minutes; For 4 servings)

**Ingredients:**

- 2 bananas, sliced into ¼ inch rounds
- 2 tablespoons creamy peanut butter

**Preparation:**

1. Add banana slices with peanut butter in a medium-sized bowl

2. Toss well until coated

3. Add water if needed

4. Arrange banana in a single layer on Crisper Basket

5. Transfer the basket to your Grill Grate

6. Preheat your Ninja Foodi Smart XL Grill by pressing the "DEHYDRATE" mode at 135 degrees F

7. Set the timer for 15 minutes

8. Let it preheat until you hear a beep

9. Once cooked, serve

10. Enjoy!

**Nutritional Values Per Serving:**

Calories: 389; Fat: 17 g; Saturated Fat: 5 g; Carbohydrates: 60 g; Fiber: 3 g; Sodium: 241 mg; Protein: 11 g

# Lovely Baked Muffin Egg

(Prep time: 5-10 minutes; Cook time: 15 minutes; For 4 servings)

## Ingredients:

- Parsley, chopped as needed
- Salt and pepper to taste
- 4 large eggs
- 4 large bell peppers, seeded and tops removed
- 4 bacon, sliced, cooked, and chopped
- 1 cup cheddar cheese, shredded

## Preparation:

1. Take your bell peppers and divide cheese and bacon between them, crack an egg into each of the bell peppers. Season them with salt and pepper

2. Preheat Ninja Foodi Smart XL by pressing the "AIR CRISP" option and setting it to "390 Degrees F" and timer to 15 minutes

3. Let it preheat until you hear a beep

4. Transfer bell pepper to your cooking basket and transfer to Foodi Grill, lock lid, and cook for 10-15 minutes until egg whites are cooked well until the yolks are slightly runny

5. Remove peppers from the basket and garnish with parsley, serve and enjoy!

## Nutritional Values Per Serving:

Calories: 326; Fat: 23 g; Saturated Fat: 10 g; Carbohydrates: 10 g; Fiber: 2 g; Sodium: 781 mg; Protein: 22 g

# Juicy Mushroom Frittata

(Prep time: 10 minutes; Cook time: 10 minutes; For 1 serving)

**Ingredients:**

- 4 cremini mushrooms, sliced
- ½ cup cheddar cheese, shredded
- 4 large eggs
- ¼ cup whole milk
- ½ bell pepper, seeded and diced
- ½ onion, chopped
- Salt and pepper, to taste

**Preparation:**

1. Add the whisked egg, milk, salt, and pepper into a medium-sized bowl
2. Add bell pepper, mushroom, cheese, and onion
3. Mix them well
4. Preheat your Ninja Foodi Smart XL Grill by pressing the "BAKE" mode at 400 degrees F
5. Set the timer for 10 minutes
6. Let it preheat until you hear a beep
7. Pour the egg mixture into your Ninja Foodi Bake pan
8. Spread the mixture evenly
9. Transfer to Grill and lock the lid
10. Bake for 10 minutes
11. Once cooked, serve
12. Enjoy!

**Nutritional Values Per Serving:**

Calories: 153; Fat: 1 g; Saturated Fat: 0 g; Carbohydrates: 5 g; Fiber: 2 g; Sodium: 0245mg; Protein: 11 g

# French Morning Toasties

(Prep time: 5-10 minutes; Cook time: 10 minutes; For 4 servings)

**Ingredients:**

- Cooking spray as needed

- 6 slices bread, sliced into strips
- ¼ teaspoon vanilla extract
- ¼ teaspoon ground cinnamon
- ¼ cup granulated sugar
- ½ cup milk
- 4 whole eggs

**Preparation:**

1. Take a bowl and beat in eggs, milk
2. Stir in sugar, vanilla, and cinnamon
3. Dip the bread in the mix
4. Preheat your Ninja Foodi Smart XL in AIR CRISP for 10 minutes at 400 degrees F
5. Transfer bread to the Foodi and cook for 3-5 minutes per side
6. Enjoy!

**Nutritional Values Per Serving:**

Calories: 183; Fat: 6 g; Saturated Fat: 2 g; Carbohydrates: 24 g; Fiber: 3 g; Sodium: 269 mg; Protein: 9 g

# Delicious Mac and Cheese

(Prep time: 5-10 minutes; Cook time: 10 minutes; For 4 servings)

**Ingredients:**

- 1 tablespoon parmesan cheese, grated
- 1 cup elbow macaroni
- 1 and ½ cheddar cheese, grated
- ½ cup broccoli
- 1 cup milk, warmed
- Salt and pepper, to taste

**Preparation:**

1. Pre-heat Ninja Foodi Smart XL by pressing the "AIR CRISP" option and setting it to 400 degrees F
2. Set the timer to 10 minutes
3. Let it preheat until you hear a beep
4. Take a pot and add water

5. Allow it to boil

6. Add macaroni and veggies and boil for 10 minutes

7. Drain the pasta and vegetable using a colander

8. Add cheese to the pasta and vegetable mixture

9. Toss them well

10. Season with salt and pepper

11. Transfer the mixture to your Foodi

12. Sprinkle some more parmesan on top

13. Cook for about 15 minutes

14. Let it cool for 10 minutes

15. Serve and enjoy!

**Nutritional Values Per Serving:**

Calories: 180; Fat: 11 g; Saturated Fat: 3 g; Carbohydrates: 14 g; Fiber: 3 g; Sodium: 287 mg; Protein: 9 g

# Sweet BBQ Chicken Meal

(Prep time: 5-10 minutes; Cook time: 40 minutes; For 4 servings)

**Ingredients:**

- Salt and pepper to taste

- 1 cup white vinegar

- ¾ cup onion, chopped

- ¼ cup tomato paste

- ¼ cup garlic, minced

- 1 cup of water

- 1 cup of soy sauce

- ¾ cup of sugar

- 6 chicken drumsticks

**Preparation:**

1. Take a Ziploc bag and add all ingredients to it

2. Marinate for at least 2 hours in your refrigerator

3. Insert the crisper basket, and close the hood

4.  Preheat Ninja Foodi Smart XL by pressing the "AIR CRISP" option at 390 degrees F for 40 minutes

5.  Place the grill pan accessory in the air fryer

6.  Flip the chicken after every 10 minutes

7.  Take a saucepan and pour the marinade into it, and heat over medium flame until sauce thickens

8.  Brush with the glaze

9.  Serve warm and enjoy!

### Nutritional Values Per Serving:

Calories: 460; Fat: 20 g; Saturated Fat: 5 g; Carbohydrates: 26 g; Fiber: 3 g; Sodium: 126 mg; Protein: 28 g

# Classic French Burrito

(Prep time: 5-10 minutes; Cook time: 5 minutes; For 2 servings)

### Ingredients:

- 2 tortillas
- ½ cup bacon, cooked crisp and crumbled
- ½ cup cheddar cheese, shredded
- 2 whole eggs, scrambled

### Preparation:

1.  Take a bowl and add eggs, bacon, and cheese

2.  Top tortillas with the mix

3.  Roll the tortillas, transfer to the Ninja Foodi Smart XL

4.  Select AIR CRISP and cook for 5 minutes at 250 degrees F

5.  Serve and enjoy!

### Nutritional Values Per Serving:

Calories: 531; Fat: 15 g; Saturated Fat: 3 g; Carbohydrates: 81 g; Fiber: 2 g; Sodium: 1125 mg; Protein: 18 g

# Excellent Rum Sundae

(Prep time: 5-10 minutes; Cook time: 8 minutes; For 4 servings)

**Ingredients:**

- ½ cup dark rum
- ½ cup brown sugar, packed
- 1 teaspoon cinnamon, ground
- 1 pineapple, cored and sliced
- Vanilla ice cream for serving

**Preparation:**

7. Take a large-sized bowl and add sugar, rum, and cinnamon

8. Add pineapple in the layer, dredge them, and coat well

9. Preheat your Ninja Foodi to MAX and set the timer to 8 minutes

10. Once you hear the beep, strain any rum from pineapple slices and transfer them to the grill grate

11. Cook for 6-8 minutes; cook in batches if needed

12. Top each ring with a scoop of ice cream and sprinkle cinnamon

13. Enjoy!

**Nutritional Values Per Serving:**

Calories: 240; Fat: 4 g; Saturated Fat: 1 g; Carbohydrates: 43 g; Fiber: 8 g; Sodium: 85 mg; Protein: 2 g

# Delightful Honey and Coconut Medley

(Prep time: 5-10 minutes; Cook time:10-308 minutes; For 4 servings)

**Ingredients:**

- Baking paper as needed
- ¼ ice cream sorbet
- 1 tablespoon lemon juice
- 1 tablespoon honey
- ½ small, fresh pineapples

**Preparation:**

10. Preheat your Ninja Foodi Smart XL to 392 degrees F in "AIR CRISP" mode; line the bottom of the basket with baking paper

11. Cut pineapple lengthwise into eight pieces, remove the peel with eyes alongside the woody trunk

12. Take a bowl and mix in lemon juice and honey, brush pineapple pieces with the mixture. Transfer to the basket. Sprinkle coconut over it

13. Push to Air Fryer and cook for 12 minutes

14. Serve and enjoy some ice cream.

15. Enjoy!

**Nutritional Values Per Serving:**

Calories: 435; Fat: 16 g; Saturated Fat: 4 g; Carbohydrates: 61 g; Fiber: 2 g; Sodium: 85 mg; Protein: 9 g

# Chapter 2: Crispy Chicken and Poultry

## Thai Chicken

(Prep time: 10 minutes; Cook time: 20 minutes; For 6 servings)

**Ingredients:**

- 2 pounds chicken thighs, skinless
- 1 tablespoon olive oil
- 1 cup tomato salsa, fire-roasted
- 1 teaspoon fresh ginger, finely grated
- ½ cup almond butter
- ¼ teaspoon red pepper flakes, crushed;   2 tablespoons fresh lime juice
- 1 tablespoon fresh basil, chopped;   1 tablespoon soy sauce

**Preparation:**

1. Select the "Grill" button on the Ninja Foodi Smart XL Grill and regulate the settings at Medium for 20 minutes.
2. Mingle chicken thighs with salsa, olive oil, almond butter, lime juice, soy sauce, ginger and red pepper flakes in a bowl and marinate for 3 hours.
3. Arrange the chicken in the Ninja Foodi when it displays "Add Food".
4. Grill for about 20 minutes, flipping once in between.
5. Dole out in a platter and serve garnished with fresh basil.

**Nutritional Values Per Serving:**

Calories: 323; Fat: 14.2g; Sat Fat: 3.4g; Carbohydrates: 2.1g; Fiber: 0.3g; Sugar: 0.6g; Protein: 44.3g

## Herbed Up Roast Chicken

(Prep time: 5-10 minutes; Cook time: 5 hours; For 6 servings)

**Ingredients:**

- 1 tablespoon pepper
- 2 tablespoon salt
- 5 sprigs thyme, chopped
- ¼ cup honey

- ¼ cup lemon juice
- 1 tablespoon canola oil
- 5 garlic cloves, crushed
- 1 whole chicken

**Preparation:**

1. Add garlic inside the chicken cavities
2. Brush chicken with a mixture of honey, lemon juice, and oil on all sides
3. Season with salt, pepper, and thyme
4. Transfer to Ninja Foodi Smart XL
5. Select Roast and cook for 5 hours at 250 degrees F
6. Serve and enjoy once done!

**Nutritional Values Per Serving:**

Calories: 280; Fat: 22 g; Saturated Fat: 6 g; Carbohydrates: 1 g; Fiber: 0 g; Sodium: 366 mg; Protein: 19 g

# Exciting Paprika Chicken

(Prep time: 5-10 minutes; Cook time: 30 minutes; For 4 servings)

**Ingredients:**

- Salt and pepper to taste
- 1 teaspoon garlic powder
- 1 tablespoon paprika, smoked
- 2 tablespoons olive oil
- 2 pounds of chicken wings

**Preparation:**

1. Take the chicken wings and coat them with oil
2. Sprinkle with paprika, garlic powder, salt, and pepper
3. Transfer the chicken wings to the Air Crisping basket
4. Set your Ninja Foodi Smart XL to AIR CRISP
5. Cook for 15 minutes per side at 400 degrees F
6. Once done, serve and enjoy!

**Nutritional Values Per Serving:**

Calories: 792; Fat: 58 g; Saturated Fat: 15 g; Carbohydrates: 2 g; Fiber: 0 g; Sodium: 721 mg; Protein: 62 g

# Herbed Roasted Chicken

(Prep time: 5 minutes; Cook time:18 minutes; For 4 servings)

**Ingredients:**

- Salt, to taste
- 4 chicken thighs, skin on, bone removed
- Black pepper, for garnish
- Garlic powder, to taste

**Preparation:**

1. Select the "Air Crisp" button on the Ninja Foodi Smart XL Grill and regulate the settings at 400 degrees F for 18 minutes.
2. Dust the chicken with garlic powder and salt.
3. Arrange the chicken in the Ninja Foodi when it displays "Add Food".
4. Air crisp for 18 minutes, flipping once in between.
5. Dole out in a platter and dust with black pepper to serve.

**Nutritional Values Per Serving:**

Calories: 140; Fat: 7.9g; Sat Fat: 1.8g; Carbohydrates: 2.6g; Fiber: 1.8g; Sugar: 1.5g; Protein: 7.2g

# Sweet Tangy Orange Chicken

(Prep time: 5-10 minutes; Cook time: 15 minutes; For 4 servings)

**Ingredients:**

- 2 teaspoons ground coriander
- ½ teaspoons garlic salt
- ¼ teaspoon ground black pepper
- 12 chicken wings
- 1 tablespoon canola oil
- ¼ cup butter, melted
- 3 tablespoons honey
- ½ cup of orange juice
- 1/3 cup Sriracha chili sauce
- 2 tablespoons lime juice

- ¼ cup cilantro, chopped

**Preparation:**

1. Take the chicken and coat them well with oil

2. Season with spices, let them sit for 2 hours in the fridge

3. Add remaining ingredients to a saucepan and cook over low heat for 3-4 minutes

4. Set your Ninja Foodi Smart XL to GRILl and MED mode

5. Set timer to 10 minutes

6. Add chicken to grill grate, cook for 5 minutes, flip and cook for 5 minutes more

7. Serve and enjoy once done!

**Nutritional Values Per Serving:**

Calories: 320; Fat: 14 g; Saturated Fat: 4 g; Carbohydrates: 19 g; Fiber: 1 g; Sodium: 258 mg; Protein: 25 g

# Orange Blossom Chicken

(Cook time:12-24 minutes; For 4 servings)

**Ingredients:**

- 2 tablespoons of orange zest

- 4 frozen boneless, skinless chicken breasts (8 ounces each)

- 2 tablespoons kosher salt

- 1 tablespoon sugar

- 1 tablespoon of avocado oil

- 1 cup cream

- 1 cup chicken broth

- 1 tablespoon instant flour

**Preparation:**

1. Insert the grill grate inside the unit and close the hood.

2. Now select the grill option and set the temperature to medium.

3. Set time to 20 minutes, for preheating.

4. Now select start and beginner preheating process.

5. Meanwhile, take a large bowl and mix chicken breast pieces with salt, sugar, almond flour, and orange zest, mix well

6. Add one tablespoon of avocado oil and rub the chicken well.

7. Once the preheating time complete and chicken is finely coated, place it on the grill grate, close the unit and cook for 6 minutes.

8. Flip the chicken and cook for 7 minutes.

9. Once done remove the chicken from the unit and let it sit for 5 minutes before cutting and serving.

**Nutritional Values Per Serving:**

Calories: 417; Fat: 11g; Carbohydrates: 7.5g; Fiber: 0.5g; Sugar: 4.4g; Protein 67.7g

# Sesame Chicken Breast

(Prep time: 5 minutes; Cook time:20 minutes; For 2 servings)

**Ingredients:**

- 2 chicken breasts
- 2 tablespoons sesame oil
- 1 teaspoon kosher salt
- ¼ teaspoon cayenne pepper
- 1 tablespoon sweet paprika
- ½ teaspoon black pepper
- 1 tablespoon onions powder
- 1 tablespoon garlic powder

**Preparation:**

1. Press the "Bake" button on the Ninja Foodi Smart XL Grill and adjust the time for 20 minutes at 380 degrees F.

2. Season the chicken breasts with sesame oil and all other spices.

3. Place the chicken in the Ninja Foodi when it shows "Add Food".

4. Bake for 20 minutes and dole out to serve warm.

**Nutritional Values Per Serving:**

Calories: 453; Fat: 2.4g; Sat Fat: 3g; Carbohydrates: 18g; Fiber: 2.3g; Sugar: 3.3g; Protein: 23.2g

# Chicken Broccoli

(Prep time: 5 minutes; Cook time:20 minutes; For 4 servings)

**Ingredients:**

- 1 pound chicken breast, boneless and cut into bite-sized pieces
- 1 tablespoon soy sauce, low sodium
- 1 tablespoon olive oil
- ½ pound broccoli, cut into small florets
- 2 teaspoons hot sauce
- ½ onion, sliced
- 1 teaspoon sesame seed oil
- Salt, to taste
- Black pepper, to taste
- ½ teaspoon garlic powder
- 1 tablespoon fresh minced ginger
- 2 teaspoons rice vinegar

**Preparation:**

1. Select the "Grill" button on the Ninja Foodi Smart XL Grill and regulate the settings at Medium for 20 minutes.
2. Mingle the chicken breasts with onion and broccoli in a bowl.
3. Throw in the remaining ingredients and toss thoroughly.
4. Arrange the chicken in the Ninja Foodi when it displays "Add Food".
5. Grill for about 20 minutes, flipping once in between.
6. Dole out in a platter and shower with lemon juice to serve.

**Nutritional Values Per Serving:**

Calories: 352; Fat: 14g; Sat Fat: 2g; Carbohydrates: 5.8g; Fiber: 0g; Sugar: 0.2g; Protein: 26g

# Teriyaki Chicken Meal

(Prep time: 5-10 minutes; Cook time: 30 minutes; For 4 servings)

**Ingredients:**

- ¼ cup teriyaki sauce
- Cooking spray as needed
- Salt and pepper to taste
- 2 chicken breast fillets, sliced into strips

**Preparation:**

1. Take the chicken strips and season them well with salt and pepper
2. Spray them with oil, transfer chicken strips to the grill grate
3. Set your Ninja Foodi Smart XL to Grill
4. Set To HIGH
5. Cook for about 5 minutes
6. Flip and cook for 5 minutes more
7. Brush the chicken with teriyaki sauce and cook for 10 minutes more, making sure to flip once
8. Serve and enjoy!

**Nutritional Values Per Serving:**

Calories: 376; Fat: 25 g; Saturated Fat: 5 g; Carbohydrates: 3 g; Fiber: 1 g; Sodium: 1358 mg; Protein: 27 g

# Teriyaki Chicken Meal

(Prep time: 5-10 minutes; Cook time:30 minutes; For 4 servings)

**Ingredients:**

- ¼ cup teriyaki sauce
- Cooking spray as needed
- Salt and pepper to taste
- 2 chicken breast fillets, sliced into strips

**Preparation:**

1. Take the chicken strips and season them well with salt and pepper
2. Spray them with oil, transfer chicken strips to the grill grate

3. Set your Ninja Foodi Smart XL to Grill

4. Set To HIGH

5. Cook for about 5 minutes

6. Flip and cook for 5 minutes more

7. Brush the chicken with teriyaki sauce and cook for 10 minutes more, making sure to flip once

8. Serve and enjoy!

**Nutritional Values Per Serving:**

Calories: 376; Fat: 25g; Sat Fat: 5g; Carbohydrates: 3g; Fiber: 1g; Sodium: 1,3g; Protein: 27g

# Excellent Coconut Touched Chicken Meal

(Prep time: 5-10 minutes; Cook time: 12 minutes; For 4 servings)

**Ingredients:**

- 2 large whole eggs
- 2 teaspoons garlic powder
- 1 teaspoon salt and ½ teaspoon pepper
- ¾ cup coconut minos
- 1 pound chicken tenders
- Cooking spray as needed

**Preparation:**

1. Set your Ninja Foodi Smart XL to AIR CRISP mode

2. Set temperature to 400 degrees F and set timer to 12 minutes

3. Take a large baking sheet and grease with cooking spray

4. Take a wide dish, add eggs, garlic, salt, and pepper, whisk well

5. Add almond meal, coconut and mix well

6. Take chicken tenders and dip them in egg mix, dip in coconut mix afterward

7. Shake any excess

8. Transfer the prepared chicken Grill, spray the tenders with a bit of oil

9. Air Fry for about 10-14 minutes until golden, serve and enjoy!

**Nutritional Values Per Serving:**

Calories: 180; Fat: 1 g; Saturated Fat: 0 g; Carbohydrates: 3 g; Fiber: 1 g; Sodium: 214 mg; Protein: 0 g

# Grilled Chicken Breasts

(Prep time: 5 minutes; Cook time:15 minutes; For 4 servings)

**Ingredients:**

- ¼ cup red wine vinegar
- 2 tablespoons dijon mustard
- ⅓ cup oil vegetable oil
- 3 tablespoons Worcestershire sauce
- 2 tablespoons lemon juice
- 1 tablespoon salt
- 1 tablespoon sugar
- 4 chicken breasts, boneless skinless
- 2 tablespoons Italian seasoning
- 1 tablespoon black pepper
- 1 teaspoon garlic powder

**Preparation:**

1. Select the "Grill" button on the Ninja Foodi Smart XL Grill and regulate the settings at Medium for 15 minutes.
2. Mingle all the ingredients in a bowl and scrub the chicken well in this marinade.
3. Arrange the chicken in the Ninja Foodi when it displays "Add Food".
4. Grill for about 15 minutes, flipping once in between.
5. Dole out in a platter and serve warm.
6. Dole out in a platter and shower with lemon juice to serve.

**Nutritional Values Per Serving:**

Calories: 238; Fat: 14g; Sat Fat: 1g; Carbohydrates: 2g; Fiber: 0.1g; Sugar: 1g; Protein: 24g

# Southern-Style Chicken

(Prep time: 5 minutes; Cook time:20 minutes; For 6 servings)

**Ingredients:**

- 2 cups Ritz crackers, crushed
- 1 tablespoon fresh parsley, minced

- 1 teaspoon garlic salt
- ¼ teaspoon rubbed sage
- 1 teaspoon paprika
- 1 large egg, beaten
- ½ teaspoon black pepper
- 1 (3-4 pounds) broiler/fryer chicken, cut up
- ¼ teaspoon ground cumin

**Preparation:**

1. Select the "Air Crisp" button on the Ninja Foodi Smart XL Grill and regulate the settings at 350 degrees F for 20 minutes.
2. Whip egg in a bowl and mingle rest of the ingredients except chicken in another bowl.
3. Immerse the chicken in the whipped egg and then dredge in the dry mixture.
4. Arrange the chicken in the Ninja Foodi when it displays "Add Food".
5. Air crisp for about 20 minutes and dole out to serve warm.

**Nutritional Values Per Serving:**

Calories: 391; Fat: 2.8g; Sat Fat: 0.6g; Carbohydrates: 16.5g; Fiber: 9.2g; Sugar: 4.2g; Protein: 26.6g

# Clean Apple Flavored Alfredo Chicken

(Prep time: 5-10 minutes; Cook time: 20 minutes; For 4 servings)

**Ingredients:**

- 1 large apple, wedged
- 1 tablespoon lemon juice
- 4 chicken breast, halved
- 4 teaspoons chicken seasoning
- 4 slices provolone cheese
- ¼ cup blue cheese, crumbled
- ½ cup alfredo sauce

**Preparation:**

1. Take a mixing bowl and add seasoning
2. Take another bowl and toss apple with lemon juice
3. Set your Ninja Foodi Smart XL to Grill and MED mode, set timer to 16 minutes
4. Transfer chicken over grill grate, lock lid, and cook for 8 minutes

5. Flip and cook for 8 minutes more
6. Grill the apple in a similar manner, 2 minutes per side
7. Serve the cooked chicken with sauce, grilled apple, and cheese
8. Enjoy!

**Nutritional Values Per Serving:**

Calories: 247; Fat: 19 g; Saturated Fat: 3 g; Carbohydrates: 29 g; Fiber: 2 g; Sodium: 850 mg; Protein: 14 g

# Juicy Grilled Chicken Breasts

(Cook time:17 minutes; For 4 servings)

## Ingredients:

- 4 chicken breasts, 8 ounces each
- 1/3 cup olive oil
- 3 tablespoon soy sauce
- 2 tablespoon balsamic vinegar
- 1/4 cup brown sugar
- 1 tablespoon Worcestershire sauce
- 3 tsp minced garlic
- Salt and black pepper, to taste

## Preparation:

1. Take a large bowl and whisk together soy sauce, vinegar, brown sugar, garlic, pepper, oil, salt, and Worcestershire sauce.
2. Take about cup of this mixture and set it aside for later serving.
3. Poke the chicken breast with a fork and soaked in the bowl marinate for 20 minutes.
4. Insert the grill grate to the unit and close the hood.
5. Now set the temperature to medium and set the timer to 10 minutes.
6. Once the grill is preheated, add chicken breast pieces into the grill and set the timer to 10 minutes.
7. After 5 minutes, open the unit and flip the chicken.
8. Cook for another 5 minutes.
9. After 5 minutes, baste the chicken with more basting liquid, cook for 2 minutes. Once done, serve and enjoy.

**Nutritional Values Per Serving:**

Calories: 391; Fat: 23.7g; Carbohydrates: 11.3g; Fiber: 0.2g; Sugar: 4.2g; Protein 66.6g

# Crispy Chicken and Potatoes

(Prep time: 5 minutes; Cook time:15 minutes; For 4 servings)

**Ingredients:**

- 15 oz can potatoes, drained
- 1 teaspoon olive oil
- 1 teaspoon Lawry's seasoned salt
- 3/8 cup cheddar cheese, shredded
- ¼ teaspoon paprika
- 8 oz chicken breast, boneless, skinless, and cubed
- 1/8 teaspoon black pepper
- 4 bacon slices, cooked and cut into strips

**Preparation:**

1. Select the "Broil" button on the Ninja Foodi Smart XL Grill and regulate the settiings for 20 minutes.
2. Scrub the chicken and potato pieces with spices and olive oil.
3. Arrange the chicken and potatoes in the Ninja Foodi when it displays "Add Food".
4. Put the bacon and cheese on the top and start broiling, flipping once in between.
5. Dole out in a platter and top with dried herbs to serve.

**Nutritional Values Per Serving:**

Calories: 301; Fat: 15.8g; Sat Fat: 2.7g; Carbohydrates: 31.7g; Fiber: 0.3g; Sugar: 6.1g; Protein: 28.2g

# Clean Apple Flavored Alfredo Chicken

(Prep time: 5-10 minutes; Cook time:20 minutes; For 4 servings)

**Ingredients:**

- 1 large apple, wedged
- 1 tablespoon lemon juice
- 4 chicken breast, halved
- 4 teaspoons chicken seasoning
- 4 slices provolone cheese
- ¼ cup blue cheese, crumbled

- ½ cup alfredo sauce

**Preparation:**

1. Take a mixing bowl and add seasoning

2. Take another bowl and toss apple with lemon juice

3. Set your Ninja Foodi Smart XL to Grill and MED mode, set timer to 16 minutes

4. Transfer chicken over grill grate, lock lid, and cook for 8 minutes

5. Flip and cook for 8 minutes more

6. Grill the apple in a similar manner, 2 minutes per side

7. Serve the cooked chicken with sauce, grilled apple, and cheese

**Nutritional Values Per Serving:**

Calories: 247; Fat: 19g; Sat Fat: 3g; Carbohydrates: 29g; Sugar: 1.5g; Protein: 14 g

# Lovely Lemon Mustard Chicken

(Prep time: 5-10 minutes; Cook time: 30 minutes; For 6 servings)

**Ingredients:**

- 6 chicken thighs

- Salt and pepper to taste

- 3 teaspoons dried Italian seasoning

- 1 tablespoon oregano, dried

- ½ cup Dijon mustard

- ¼ cup of vegetable oil

- 2 tablespoons lemon juice

**Preparation:**

1. Take a bowl and add all listed ingredients except chicken

2. Mix everything well

3. Brush both sides of the chicken with the mixture, transfer chicken to the cooking basket

4. Set your Ninja Foodi Smart XL to roast mode, set temperature to 350 degrees F

5. Select chicken mode and start; let it cook until the timer runs out

6. Serve and enjoy!

**Nutritional Values Per Serving:**

Calories: 797; Fat: 52 g; Saturated Fat: 20 g; Carbohydrates: 45 g; Fiber: 9 g; Sodium: 1566 mg; Protein: 42 g

# Exciting Paprika Chicken

(Prep time: 5-10 minutes; Cook time:30 minutes; For 4 servings)

**Ingredients:**

- Salt and pepper to taste
- 1 teaspoon garlic powder
- 1 tablespoon paprika, smoked
- 2 tablespoons olive oil
- 2 pounds of chicken wings

**Preparation:**

1. Take the chicken wings and coat them with oil
2. Sprinkle with paprika, garlic powder, salt, and pepper
3. Transfer the chicken wings to the Air Crisping basket
4. Set your Ninja Foodi Smart XL to AIR CRISP
5. Cook for 15 minutes per side at 400 degrees F
6. Once done, serve and enjoy!

**Nutritional Values Per Serving:**

Calories: 792; Fat: 58g; Sat Fat: 15g; Carbohydrates: 2g; Fiber: 0g; Sugar: 58g; Protein: 62g

# Southern-Style Chicken

(Prep time: 5 minutes; Cook time:20 minutes; For 6 servings)

**Ingredients:**

- 2 cups Ritz crackers, crushed
- 1 tablespoon fresh parsley, minced
- 1 teaspoon garlic salt
- ¼ teaspoon rubbed sage
- 1 teaspoon paprika
- 1 large egg, beaten
- ½ teaspoon black pepper
- 1 (3-4 pounds) broiler/fryer chicken, cut up
- ¼ teaspoon ground cumin

**Preparation:**

1. Select the "Air Crisp" button on the Ninja Foodi Smart XL Grill and regulate the settings at 350 degrees F for 20 minutes.
2. Whip egg in a bowl and mingle rest of the ingredients except chicken in another bowl.
3. Immerse the chicken in the whipped egg and then dredge in the dry mixture.
4. Arrange the chicken in the Ninja Foodi when it displays "Add Food".
5. Air crisp for about 20 minutes and dole out to serve warm.

**Nutritional Values Per Serving:**

Calories: 391; Fat: 2.8g; Sat Fat: 0,6g; Carbohydrates: 16.5g

# Excellent Coconut Touched Chicken Meal

(Prep time: 5-10 minutes; Cook time: 12 minutes; For 4 servings)

**Ingredients:**

- 2 large whole eggs
- 2 teaspoons garlic powder
- 1 teaspoon salt and ½ teaspoon pepper
- ¾ cup coconut minos
- 1 pound chicken tenders
- Cooking spray as needed

**Preparation:**

1. Set your Ninja Foodi Smart XL to AIR CRISP mode
2. Set temperature to 400 degrees F and set timer to 12 minutes
3. Take a large baking sheet and grease with cooking spray
4. Take a wide dish, add eggs, garlic, salt, and pepper, whisk well
5. Add almond meal, coconut and mix well
6. Take chicken tenders and dip them in egg mix, dip in coconut mix afterward
7. Shake any excess
8. Transfer the prepared chicken Grill, spray the tenders with a bit of oil
9. Air Fry for about 10-14 minutes until golden, serve and enjoy!

**Nutritional Values Per Serving:**

Calories: 180; Fat: 1g; Carbohydrates: 3g; Fiber: 1g; Sodium 214 mg

# Chapter 3: Fresh Fish and Seafood

## Seasoned Catfish

(Prep time: 10 minutes; Cook time:20 minutes; For 4 servings)

**Ingredients:**

- 4 (4-ounce) catfish fillets
- ¼ cup Louisiana fish fry seasoning
- 1 tablespoon olive oil
- 1 tablespoon fresh parsley, chopped

**Preparation:**

1. Rub the fish fillets with seasoning generously and then, coat with oil.
2. Arrange the greased "Crisper Basket" in the pot of Ninja Foodi Grill.
3. Close the Ninja Foodi Grill with lid and select "Air Crisp".
4. Set the temperature to 400 degrees F to preheat.
5. Press "Start/Stop" to begin preheating.
6. When the display shows "Add Food" open the lid and place the fish fillets into the "Crisper Basket".
7. Close the Ninja Foodi Grill with lid and set the time for 20 minutes.
8. Press "Start/Stop" to begin cooking.
9. After 10 minutes of cooking, flip the fish fillets.
10. When the Cook time is completed, press "Start/Stop" to stop cooking and open the lid.
11. Serve hot with the garnishing of parsley.

**Nutritional Values Per Serving:**

Calories: 213; Fat: 12.1g; Saturated Fat: 2.1g; Carbohydrates: 7.6g; Sugar: 0g; Protein: 17.7g

## Lemon Pepper White Fish

(Cook time:20 minutes; For 2 servings)

**Ingredients:**

- 12 oz white fish fillets
- 1/2 tsp lemon pepper seasoning

- 1/2 tsp garlic powder
- 1/2 tsp onion powder
- Pepper
- Salt

**Preparation:**

1. Spray fish fillets with cooking spray and season with lemon pepper seasoning, garlic powder, onion powder, pepper, and salt.
2. Place the cooking pot in the unit then place the crisper basket in the pot and close the hood.
3. Select air crisp mode then set the temperature to 360 F and set the timer to 10 minutes. Press start to begin preheating.
4. Once the unit is preheated it will beep then place fish fillets in the basket. Close the hood.
5. Cook fish fillets for 10 minutes.
6. Serve and enjoy.

**Nutritional Values Per Serving:**

Calories 295; Fat 12 g; Carbohydrates 1.4 g; Sugar 0.4 g; Protein 42 g; Cholesterol 131 mg

# Tuna Patties

(Cook time:30 minutes; For 8 servings)

**Ingredients:**

- 12 oz can tuna, drained
- 3 egg yolks
- 1/3 cup almond flour
- 1 zucchini, shredded and squeeze out all liquid
- 1 tsp garlic powder
- 1 tsp onion powder
- Salt

**Preparation:**

1. Add all ingredients into the mixing bowl and mix until well combined.
2. Make patties from the mixture.

3. Place the cooking pot in the unit then place the crisper basket in the pot and close the hood.

4. Select air crisp mode then set the temperature to 350 F and set the timer to 20 minutes. Press start to begin preheating.

5. Once the unit is preheated it will beep then place patties in the basket. Close the hood.

6. Cook patties for 20 minutes. Turn patties halfway through.

7. Serve and enjoy.

**Nutritional Values Per Serving:**

Calories 85; Fat 3 g; Carbohydrates 1.8 g; Sugar 0.7 g; Protein 13 g; Cholesterol 91 mg

# Flavorful Grilled Cod

(Cook time: 18 minutes; For 4 servings)

## Ingredients:

- 4 cod fillets
- 2 tbsp blackened seasoning
- 1 tbsp olive oil
- ½ tsp kosher salt

## Preparation:

1. Brush cod fillets with oil and season with blackened seasoning and kosher salt.

2. Place the cooking pot in the unit then place the grill grate in the pot and close the hood.

3. Select grill mode then set the temperature to medium and set the timer to 8 minutes. Press start to begin preheating.

4. Once the unit is preheated it will beep then place cod fillets on grill grates and close the hood.

5. Cook fish fillets for 4 minutes then flip fish fillets and continue cooking for 4 minutes.

6. Serve and enjoy.

**Nutritional Values Per Serving:**

Calories 150; Fat 4 g; Carbohydrates 19 g; Sugar 0 g; Protein 10 g; Cholesterol 15 mg

# Easy Lemon Pepper Salmon

(Cook time:18 minutes; For 4 servings)

**Ingredients:**

- 1 ½ lbs salmon fillets
- 1 tsp dried oregano
- 2 garlic cloves, minced
- ¼ cup olive oil
- 1 lemon juice
- ½ tsp pepper
- 1 tsp sea salt

**Preparation:**

1. In a large bowl, mix oregano, garlic, oil, lemon juice, pepper, and salt. Add salmon fillets and coat well. Cover and place in the refrigerator for 15 minutes.
2. Place the cooking pot in the unit then place the grill grate in the pot and close the hood.
3. Select grill mode then set the temperature to medium and set the timer to 8 minutes. Press start to begin preheating.
4. Once the unit is preheated it will beep then place marinated fish fillets on grill grates and close the hood.
5. Cook fish fillets for 4 minutes then flip fish fillets and continue cooking for 4 minutes.
6. Serve and enjoy.

**Nutritional Values Per Serving:**

Calories 337; Fat 23.2 g; Carbohydrates 0.9 g; Sugar 0 g; Protein 33.2 g; Cholesterol 75 mg

# Salmon Patties

(Cook time:18 minutes; For 6 servings)

**Ingredients:**

- 2 eggs
- 1 lb salmon fillet, remove skin
- 1 tsp mustard
- 1 tbsp fresh lemon juice
- ¼ cup mayonnaise

- ¼ cup fresh parsley, chopped
- 1 cup breadcrumbs
- ½ tsp pepper
- ½ tsp salt

**Preparation:**

1. Add all ingredients into the bowl and mix until well combined. Make 6 equal shapes of patties from the mixture.
2. Place the cooking pot in the unit then place the grill grate in the pot and close the hood.
3. Select grill mode then set the temperature to medium and set the timer to 8 minutes. Press start to begin preheating.
4. Once the unit is preheated it will beep then place patties on grill grates and close the hood.
5. Cook patties for 4 minutes then flip patties and continue cooking for 4 minutes.
6. Serve and enjoy.

**Nutritional Values Per Serving:**

Calories 235; Fat 10.6 g; Carbohydrates 15.9 g; Sugar 2 g; Protein 19.3 g; Cholesterol 90 mg

# Glazed Salmon

(Prep time: 10 minutes; Cook time:13 minutes; For 2 servings)

**Ingredients:**

- 3 tablespoons low-sodium soy sauce
- 2 tablespoons maple syrup
- 2 teaspoons fresh lemon juice
- 2 teaspoons water
- 2 (4-ounce) salmon fillets

**Preparation:**

1. Place all the ingredients in a small bowl except the salmon and mix well.
2. In a small bowl, reserve about half of the mixture.
3. Add the salmon in the remaining mixture and coat well.
4. Refrigerate, covered to marinate for about 2 hours.
5. Arrange the "Crisper Basket" in the pot of Ninja Foodi Grill
6. Close the Ninja Foodi Grill with lid and select "Air Crisp".

7. Set the temperature to 355 degrees F to preheat.

8. Press "Start/Stop" to begin preheating.

9. When the display shows "Add Food" open the lid and place the salmon fillets into the "Crisper Basket" in a single layer.

10. Close the Ninja Foodi Grill with lid and set the time for 13 minutes.

11. Press "Start/Stop" to begin cooking.

12. After 8 minutes, flip the salmon fillets and coat with reserved marinade.

13. When the Cook time is completed, press "Start/Stop" to stop cooking and open the lid.

14. Serve hot.

**Nutritional Values Per Serving:**

Calories: 211; Fat: 7.1g; Saturated Fat: 1.1g; Carbohydrates: 15g; Sugar: 13.5g; Protein: 23.5g

# Cajun Shrimp

(Cook time: 20 minutes; For 4 servings)

## Ingredients:

- 1 lb shrimp, peeled and deveined
- 1/2 tsp Cajun seasoning
- 1 garlic clove, minced
- 1 tbsp olive oil
- Pepper
- Salt

## Preparation:

1. Add shrimp, oil, Cajun seasoning, garlic, pepper, and salt into the bowl. Toss well and place in the refrigerator for 1 hour.

2. Place the cooking pot in the unit then place the crisper basket in the pot and close the hood.

3. Select air crisp mode then set the temperature to 350 F and set the timer to 10 minutes. Press start to begin preheating.

4. Once the unit is preheated it will beep then place shrimp in the basket. Close the hood.

5. Cook shrimp for 10 minutes.

6. Serve and enjoy.

## Nutritional Values Per Serving:

Calories 165; Fat 5.4 g; Carbohydrates 2 g; Sugar 0 g; Protein 26 g; Cholesterol 239 mg

# Buttered Trout

(Prep time: 10 minutes; Cook time:10 minutes; For 2 servings)

**Ingredients:**

- 2 (6-ounces) trout fillets
- Salt and freshly ground black pepper, to taste
- 1 tablespoon butter, melted

**Preparation:**

1. Season each trout fillet with salt and black pepper and then coat with the butter.
2. Arrange the trout fillets into q greased baking pan in a single layer.
3. Arrange the "Crisper Basket" in the pot of Ninja Foodi Grill.
4. Close the Ninja Foodi Grill with lid and select "Air Crisp".
5. Set the temperature to 360 degrees F to preheat.
6. Press "Start/Stop" to begin preheating.
7. When the display shows "Add Food" open the lid and place the pan into the "Crisper Basket".
8. Close the Ninja Foodi Grill with lid and set the time for 10 minutes.
9. Press "Start/Stop" to begin cooking.
10. Flip the fillets once halfway through.
11. When the Cook time is completed, press "Start/Stop" to stop cooking and open the lid.
12. Serve hot.

**Nutritional Values Per Serving:**

Calories: 374; Fat: 20.2g; Saturated Fat: 6.2g; Carbohydrates: 0g; Sugar: 0g; Protein: 45.4g

# Easy Salmon Patties

(Cook time:17 minutes; For 2 servings)

**Ingredients:**

- 8 oz salmon fillet, minced
- 1 egg, lightly beaten
- 1/4 tsp garlic powder
- 1/8 tsp salt

## Preparation:

1. In a bowl, mix salmon, garlic powder, egg, and salt until well combined.

2. Make two patties from the salmon mixture.

3. Place the cooking pot in the unit then place the crisper basket in the pot and close the hood.

4. Select air crisp mode then set the temperature to 390 F and set the timer to 7 minutes. Press start to begin preheating.

5. Once the unit is preheated it will beep then place patties in the basket. Close the hood.

6. Cook salmon patties for 7 minutes.

7. Serve and enjoy.

## Nutritional Values Per Serving:

Calories 190; Fat 9.3 g; Carbohydrates 3.1 g; Sugar 1 g; Protein 25.2 g; Cholesterol 132 mg

# Crispy Cod

(Prep time: 15 minutes; Cook time:15 minutes; For 4 servings)

## Ingredients:

- 4 (4-ounce) (¾-inch thick) cod fillets
- Salt, to taste
- 2 tablespoons all-purpose flour
- 2 eggs
- ½ cup panko breadcrumbs
- 1 teaspoon fresh dill, minced
- ½ teaspoon dry mustard
- ½ teaspoon lemon zest, grated
- ½ teaspoon onion powder
- ½ teaspoon paprika
- Olive oil cooking spray

## Preparation:

1. Season the cod fillets with salt pepper generously.

2. In a shallow bowl, place the flour.

3. Crack the eggs in a second bowl and beat well.

4. In a third bowl, mix together the panko, dill, lemon zest, mustard and spices.

5. Coat each cod fillet with the flour, then dip into beaten eggs and finally, coat with panko mixture.

6. Arrange the greased "Crisper Basket" in the pot of Ninja Foodi Grill.

7. Close the Ninja Foodi Grill with lid and select "Air Crisp".

8. Set the temperature to 400 degrees F to preheat.

9. Press "Start/Stop" to begin preheating.

10.  When the display shows "Add Food" open the lid and place the cod fillets into the "Crisper Basket".

11. Spray the cod fillets with cooking spray.

12. Close the Ninja Foodi Grill with lid and set the time for 15 minutes.

13. Press "Start/Stop" to begin cooking.

14. While cooking, flip the cod fillets once halfway through and spray with cooking spray.

15. When the Cook time is completed, press "Start/Stop" to stop cooking and open the lid.

16. Serve hot.

**Nutritional Values Per Serving:**

Calories: 190; Fat: 4.3g; Saturated Fat: 1.1g; Carbohydrates: 5.9 g; Sugar: 0.4g; Protein: 24g

# Buttered Scallops

(Prep time: 15 minutes; Cook time:6 minutes; For 6 servings)

**Ingredients:**

- ½ cup butter
- 4 garlic cloves, minced
- 1 tablespoon fresh rosemary, chopped
- 1 tablespoon fresh thyme, chopped
- 2 pounds sea scallops
- Salt and freshly ground black pepper, to taste

**Preparation:**

1. In a skillet, melt the butter over medium heat and sauté the garlic and rosemary for about 1 minute.

2. Stir in the scallops, salt and black pepper and cook for about 2 minutes.

3. Remove from the heat and place the scallop mixture into a baking pan.

4. Arrange the greased "Crisper Basket" in the pot of Ninja Foodi Grill.

5. Close the Ninja Foodi Grill with lid and select "Air Crisp".

6. Set the temperature to 350 degrees F to preheat.

7. Press "Start/Stop" to begin preheating.

8. When the display shows "Add Food" open the lid and place the pan into the "Crisper Basket".

9. Close the Ninja Foodi Grill with lid and set the time for 3 minutes.

10. Press "Start/Stop" to begin cooking.

11. When Cook time is completed, press "Start/Stop" to stop cooking and open the lid.

12. Serve hot.

## Nutritional Values Per Serving:

Calories: 275; Fat: 16.6g; Saturated Fat: 9.9g; Carbohydrates: 4.9g; Sugar: 0g; Protein: 25.7g

# Oat Crusted Salmon

(Prep time: 15 minutes; Cook time:15 minutes; For 2 servings)

## Ingredients:

- 2 (6-ounce) skinless salmon fillets
- Salt and freshly ground black pepper, to taste
- 3 tablespoons walnuts, chopped finely
- 3 tablespoons quick-cooking oats, crushed
- 2 tablespoons olive oil

## Preparation:

1. Rub the salmon fillets with salt and black pepper evenly.

2. In a bowl, mix together the walnuts, oats and oil.

3. Arrange the salmon fillets into the greased baking pan in a single layer.

4. Place the oat mixture over salmon fillets and gently press down.

5. Arrange the "Crisper Basket" in the pot of Ninja Foodi Grill.

6. Close the Ninja Foodi Grill with lid and select "Bake".

7. Set the temperature to 400 degrees F to preheat.

8. Press "Start/Stop" to begin preheating.

9. When the display shows "Add Food" open the lid and place the pan into the "Crisper Basket".

10. Close the Ninja Foodi Grill with lid and set the time for 15 minutes.

11. Press "Start/Stop" to begin cooking.

12. When the Cook time is completed, press "Start/Stop" to stop cooking and open the lid.

13. Serve hot.

**Nutritional Values Per Serving:**

Calories: 446; Fat: 31.9g; Saturated Fat: 4g; Carbohydrates: 6.4g; Sugar: 0.2g; Protein: 36.8g

# Spiced Tilapia

(Prep time: 0 minutes; Cook time:12 minutes; For 2 servings)

## Ingredients:

- ½ teaspoon lemon pepper seasoning
- ½ teaspoon garlic powder
- 1/2 teaspoon onion powder
- Salt and freshly ground black pepper, to taste
- 2 (6-ounce) tilapia fillets
- 1 tablespoon olive oil

## Preparation:

1. In a small bowl, mix together the spices, salt and black pepper.

2. Coat the tilapia fillets with oil and then rub with spice mixture.

3. Arrange the greased "Crisper Basket" in the pot of Ninja Foodi Grill.

4. Close the Ninja Foodi Grill with lid and select "Air Crisp".

5. Set the temperature to 360 degrees F to preheat.

6. Press "Start/Stop" to begin preheating.

7. When the display shows "Add Food" open the lid and place the tilapia fillets into the "Crisper Basket".

8. Close the Ninja Foodi Grill with lid and set the time for 12 minutes.

9. Press "Start/Stop" to begin cooking.

10. Flip the fillets once halfway through.

11. When the Cook time is completed, press "Start/Stop" to stop cooking and open the lid.

12. Serve hot.

**Nutritional Values Per Serving:**

Calories: 206; Fat: 8.6g; Saturated Fat: 1.7g; Carbohydrates: 1.3g; Sugar: 0.4g; Protein: 31.9g

# Perfect Grilled Mahi Mahi

(Cook time:20 minutes; For 3 servings)

**Ingredients:**

- 3 mahi-mahi fillets
- 2 tbsp fresh lemon juice
- 1 tsp cumin
- 1 tsp dried oregano
- 1/8 tsp cayenne pepper
- ½ tsp onion powder
- ½ tsp garlic powder
- 1 tsp paprika
- 3 tbsp olive oil
- ¼ tsp pepper
- ½ tsp salt

**Preparation:**

1. In a small bowl, mix cumin, oregano, cayenne, garlic powder, paprika, pepper, and salt.
2. Brush fish fillets with oil and season with spice mixture.
3. Place the cooking pot in the unit then place the grill grate in the pot and close the hood.
4. Select grill mode then set the temperature to medium and set the timer to 10 minutes. Press start to begin preheating.
5. Once the unit is preheated it will beep then place fish fillets on grill grates and close the hood.
6. Cook fish fillets for 5 minutes then flip fish fillets and continue cooking for 5 minutes.
7. Drizzle fish fillets with lemon juice and serve.

**Nutritional Values Per Serving:**

Calories 162; Fat 14.4 g; Carbohydrates 2.1 g; Sugar 0.6 g; Protein 7.5 g; Cholesterol 13 mg

# Old Bay Seasoned Shrimp

(Cook time:16 minutes; For 2 servings)

**Ingredients:**

- 1/2 lb shrimp, peeled and deveined
- 1/2 tsp old bay seasoning
- 1/2 tsp cayenne pepper
- 1 tbsp olive oil
- 1/4 tsp paprika
- Pinch of salt

**Preparation:**

1. Add shrimp and remaining ingredients into the mixing bowl and toss well to coat.
2. Place the cooking pot in the unit then place the crisper basket in the pot and close the hood.
3. Select air crisp mode then set the temperature to 390 F and set the timer to 6 minutes. Press start to begin preheating.
4. Once the unit is preheated it will beep then place shrimp in the basket. Close the hood.
5. Cook shrimp for 6 minutes.
6. Serve and enjoy.

**Nutritional Values Per Serving:**

Calories 195; Fat 9 g; Carbohydrates 2 g; Sugar 0.1 g; Protein 26 g; Cholesterol 239 mg

# Herb Tilapia

(Cook time:20 minutes; For 2 servings)

**Ingredients:**

- 10 oz tilapia fillets
- 2 tsp fresh chives, chopped
- 2 tsp olive oil
- 1 tsp garlic, minced
- 2 tsp fresh parsley, chopped
- Pepper
- Salt

**Preparation:**

1. In a small bowl, mix oil, parsley, garlic, pepper, chives, and salt.

2. Brush oil mixture over tilapia fillets.

3. Place the cooking pot in the unit then place the crisper basket in the pot and close the hood.

4. Select air crisp mode then set the temperature to 400 F and set the timer to 10 minutes. Press start to begin preheating.

5. Once the unit is preheated it will beep then place tilapia fillets in the basket. Close the hood.

6. Cook fish fillets for 10 minutes.

7. Serve and enjoy.

**Nutritional Values Per Serving:**

Calories 182; Fat 6.2 g; Carbohydrates 0.6 g; Sugar 0 g; Protein 32 g; Cholesterol 83 mg

# Sweet & Spicy Meatballs

(Prep time: 20 minutes; Cook time: 30 minutes; For 8 servings)

**Ingredients:**

**For Meatballs:**

- 2 pounds lean ground lamb
- 2/3 cup quick-cooking oats
- ½ cup Ritz crackers, crushed
- 1 (5-ounce) can evaporated milk
- 2 large eggs, beaten lightly
- 1 teaspoon honey
- 1 tablespoon dried onion, minced
- 1 teaspoon garlic powder
- 1 teaspoon ground cumin
- Salt and freshly ground black pepper, to taste

**For Sauce:**

- 1/3 cup orange marmalade
- 1/3 cup honey
- 1/3 cup brown sugar

- 2 tablespoons cornstarch
- 2 tablespoons soy sauce
- 1-2 tablespoons hot sauce
- 1 tablespoon Worcestershire sauce

**Preparation:**

1. For meatballs: in a large bowl, add all the ingredients and mix until well combined.
2. Make 1½-inch balls from the mixture.
3. Arrange the meatballs onto a baking pan in a single layer.
4. Arrange the "Crisper Basket" in the pot of Ninja Foodi Grill.
5. Close the Ninja Foodi Grill with lid and select "Air Crisp".
6. Set the temperature to 380 degrees F to preheat.
7. Press "Start/Stop" to begin preheating.
8. When the display shows "Add Food" open the lid and place the pan into the "Crisper Basket".
9. Close the Ninja Foodi Grill with lid and set the time for 15 minutes.
10. Press "Start/Stop" to begin cooking.
11. Flip the meatballs once halfway through.
12. Meanwhile, for sauce: in a small pan, add all the ingredients over medium heat and cook until thickened, stirring continuously.
13. When the Cook time is completed, press "Start/Stop" to stop cooking and open the lid.
14. Serve the meatballs with the topping of sauce.

**Nutritional Values Per Serving:**

Calories: 413; Fat: 11.9g; Saturated Fat: 4.3g; Carbohydrates: 39.5g; Sugar: 28.2g; Protein: 36.2g

# Herbed Halibut

(Prep time: 10 minutes; Cook time: 10 minutes; For 2 servings)

**Ingredients:**

- 1 tablespoon fresh lime juice
- ½ tablespoons olive oil
- Salt and freshly ground black pepper, to taste
- 1 garlic clove, minced

- ½ teaspoon fresh thyme leaves, chopped
- ½ teaspoon fresh rosemary, chopped
- 2 (7-ounce) halibut fillets

**Preparation:**

1. In a bowl, add all the ingredients except the halibut fillets and mix well.
2. Add the halibut fillets and coat with the mixture generously.
3. Arrange the "Crisper Basket" in the pot of Ninja Foodi Grill.
4. Close the Ninja Foodi Grill with lid and select "Bake".
5. Set the temperature to 400 degrees F to preheat.
6. Press "Start/Stop" to begin preheating.
7. When the display shows "Add Food" open the lid and place the halibut fillets into the "Crisper Basket".
8. Close the Ninja Foodi Grill with lid and set the time for 10 minutes.
9. Press "Start/Stop" to begin cooking.
10. Flip the fillets once halfway through.
11. When the Cook time is completed, press "Start/Stop" to stop cooking and open the lid.
12. Serve hot.

**Nutritional Values Per Serving:**

Calories: 255; Fat: 8.2g; Saturated Fat: 1.1g; Carbohydrates: 0.9g; Sugar: 0g; Protein: 41.9g

# Quick & Easy Cajun Scallops

(Cook time:16 minutes; For 1 servings)

**Ingredients:**

- 6 scallops, clean and pat dry with a paper towel
- 1/2 tsp Cajun seasoning
- Salt

**Preparation:**

1. Season scallops with Cajun seasoning and salt.
2. Place the cooking pot in the unit then place the crisper basket in the pot and close the hood.
3. Select air crisp mode then set the temperature to 400 F and set the timer to 6 minutes. Press start to begin preheating.

4. Once the unit is preheated it will beep then place scallops in the basket. Close the hood.

5. Cook scallops for 6 minutes. Turn scallops halfway through.

6. Serve and enjoy.

**Nutritional Values Per Serving:**

Calories 155; Fat 1.4 g; Carbohydrates 4.3 g; Sugar 0 g; Protein 30 g; Cholesterol 59 mg

# Parmesan Shrimp

(Prep time: 15 minutes; Cook time:20 minutes; For 4 servings)

**Ingredients:**

- 2/3 cup Parmesan cheese, grated
- 4 garlic cloves, minced
- 2 tablespoons olive oil
- 1 teaspoon dried basil
- ½ teaspoon dried oregano
- 1 teaspoon onion powder
- ½ teaspoon red pepper flakes, crushed
- Freshly ground black pepper, to taste
- 2 pounds shrimp, peeled and deveined
- 1-2 tablespoons fresh lemon juice

**Preparation:**

1. In a large bowl, add the Parmesan cheese, garlic, oil, herbs, and spices and mix well

2. Add the shrimp and toss to coat well.

3. Arrange the greased "Crisper Basket" in the pot of Ninja Foodi Grill.

4. Close the Ninja Foodi Grill with lid and select "Air Crisp".

5. Set the temperature to 350 degrees F to preheat.

6. Press "Start/Stop" to begin preheating.

7. When the display shows "Add Food" open the lid and place half of the shrimp into the "Crisper Basket" in a single layer.

8. Close the Ninja Foodi Grill with lid and set the time for 10 minutes.

9. Press "Start/Stop" to begin cooking.

10. When the Cook time is completed, press "Start/Stop" to stop cooking and open the lid.

11. Transfer the shrimp onto a platter.

12. Repeat with the remaining shrimp.

13. Drizzle with lemon juice and serve immediately.

**Nutritional Values Per Serving:**

Calories: 386; Fat: 14.2g; Saturated Fat: 3.8g; Carbohydrates: 5. g; Sugar: 0.4g; Protein: 57.3g

# Flavorful Crab Cakes

(Cook time:20 minutes; For 5 servings)

## Ingredients:

- 2 eggs
- 1 tsp old bay seasoning
- 1 1/2 tbsp Dijon mustard
- 2 1/2 tbsp mayonnaise
- 18 oz can lump crab meat, drained
- 1/4 cup almond flour
- 2 tsp dried parsley
- 1 tbsp dried celery
- 1/2 tsp salt

## Preparation:

1. Add all ingredients into the mixing bowl and mix until well combined. Place mixture in the refrigerator for 10 minutes.

2. Make five patties from the mixture.

3. Place the cooking pot in the unit then place the crisper basket in the pot and close the hood.

4. Select air crisp mode then set the temperature to 320 F and set the timer to 10 minutes. Press start to begin preheating.

5. Once the unit is preheated it will beep then place patties in the basket. Close the hood.

6. Cook patties for 10 minutes. Turn patties halfway through.

7. Serve and enjoy.

## Nutritional Values Per Serving:

Calories 140; Fat 13 g; Carbohydrates 4.2 g; Sugar 0.7 g; Protein 17.6 g; Cholesterol 125 mg

# Chapter 4: Juicy Pork, Lamb and Beef

## Grilled Beef Burgers

(Prep time: 5-10 minutes; Cook time:10 minutes; For 4 servings)

**Ingredients:**

- 2 pounds beef, grounded
- 4 hamburger buns
- 4 slices pepper jack cheese
- 2 jalapeno peppers, seeded, stemmed and minced
- 1/2 cup shredded cheddar cheese
- 1/2 teaspoon chili powder
- 4 ounces cream cheese
- 4 slices bacon, cooked and crumbled
- 1/4 teaspoon paprika
- 1/4 teaspoon black pepper, ground
- Lettuce, sliced tomato and red onion, optional

**Preparation:**

1. Take a mixing bowl, combine with bacon, cream cheese, cheddar cheese and pepper

2. Prepare the ground beef into 8 patties

3. Add the cheese mixture onto four patties and arrange a second patty on the top of each burger, then press gently

4. all the ingredients and combine them well

5. Prepare 4 patties from the mixture

6. Take a pot, arrange reversible rack and place the crisping basket over the rack

7. Add the patties in the basket

8. Seal your ninja foodi lid

9. Pre-heat Ninja Foodi by pressing the "GRILL" option and setting it to "MED" and timer to 6 minutes

10. Let it pre-heat until you hear a beep

11. Arrange the shrimps over the grill grate, lock lid and cook for 3 minutes

12. Flip the salmon and cook for 3 minutes more

13. Serve and enjoy!

**Nutritional Values Per Serving:**

Calories: 253 kcal, Carbs: 22.5 g, Fat: 7.5 g. Protein: 36.5 g

# Beef with Pesto

(Prep time: 10 minutes; Cook time: 14 minutes; For 4 servings)

**Ingredients:**

- 4 beef(6 ounces) tenderloin steak
- 10 ounces baby spinach, chopped
- 4 cups penne pasta, uncooked
- 4 cups grape tomatoes, halved
- 1/2 cup walnuts, chopped
- 2/3 cup pesto
- 1/2 cup feta cheese, crumbled
- 1/2 teaspoon salt
- 1/2 teaspoon pepper

**Preparation:**

1. Prepare the pasta as per the given instructions on the pack
2. Drain and rinse, then keep this pasta aside
3. Season the tenderloin steaks with salt and pepper
4. Pre-heat Ninja Foodi by pressing the "GRILL" option and setting it to "HIGH" for 7 minutes
5. Once it pre-heat until you hear a beep, open the lid
6. Place the steaks in the grill grate and cook for 7 minutes
7. Flip it and cook for 7 minutes
8. Take a bowl and toss the pasta with spinach, tomatoes, walnuts, and pesto
9. Garnish with cheese
10. Serve and enjoy!

**Nutritional Values Per Serving:**

Calories: 361 kcal, Carbs: 16 g, Fat: 5 g. Protein: 33.3 g

# Authentic Korean Chili Pork

(Prep time: 10 minutes; Cook time:8 minutes; For 4 servings)

**Ingredients:**

- 2 pounds pork, cut into 1/8-inch slices
- 5 garlic cloves, minced
- 3 tablespoons green onion, minced
- 1 yellow onion, sliced
- 1/2 cup of soy sauce
- 1/2 cup brown sugar
- 3 tablespoons Korean Red Chili Paste
- 2 tablespoons sesame seeds
- 3 teaspoons black pepper
- Red pepper flakes

**Preparation:**

1. Take a zip bag and add listed ingredients, shake well and let it chill for 6-8 hours

2. Pre-heat Ninja Foodi by pressing the "GRILL" option and setting it to "MED" and timer to 8 minutes

3. Let it pre-heat until you hear a beep

4. Arrange sliced pork over grill grate, lock lid and cook for 4 minutes

5. Flip pork and cook for 4 minutes more, serve warm and enjoy with some chopped lettuce

**Nutritional Values Per Serving:**

Calories: 620 kcal, Carbs: 29 g, Fat: 31 g. Protein: 58 g

# Chili-Espresso Marinated Steak

(Prep time: 5 minutes; Cook time:50 minutes; For 3 servings)

**Ingredients:**

- 1 and 1/2 pounds beef flank steak
- 1 teaspoon instant espresso powder
- 1/2 teaspoon garlic powder
- 2 teaspoons chili powder

- 2 tablespoons olive oil
- Salt and pepper, to taste

**Preparation:**

1. Insert the grill grate and close the hood
2. Pre-heat Ninja Foodi by pressing the "GRILL" option at and setting it to "HIGH" and timer to 40 minutes
3. Once it pre-heat until you hear a beep
4. Make the dry rub by mixing the chili powder, espresso powder, garlic powder, salt, and pepper
5. Rub all over the steak and brush with oil
6. Place on the grill grate and cook for 40 minutes
7. Flip after 20 minutes
8. Serve and enjoy!

**Nutritional Values Per Serving:**

Calories: 249 kcal, Carbs: 6 g, Fat: 14 g. Protein: 20 g

# Cheese Burger

(Prep time: 10 minutes; Cook time: 20 minutes; For 2 servings)

**Ingredients:**

- 1/2 pound ground beef
- 1/4 cup cheddar cheese, shredded
- 3 tablespoons chili sauce, divided
- 1/2 tablespoon chili powder
- 2 hamburger buns, split
- Lettuce leaves, mayonnaise, tomato slices

**Preparation:**

1. Take all the ingredients for patties in a bowl
2. Mix them and then make 2 of the ½ inch patties out of it
3. Pre-heat Ninja Foodi by pressing the "GRILL" option and setting it to "HIGH"
4. Once it pre-heat until you hear a beep, open the lid
5. Place 2 patties in the grill grate and cook for 5 minutes
6. Serve with buns, tomato, lettuce and mayonnaise
7. Enjoy!

**Nutritional Values Per Serving:**

Calories: 537 kcal, Carbs: 10 g, Fat: 19.8 g. Protein: 37.8 g

# Beef Ribeye Steak

(Prep time: 5 minutes; Cook time: 20 minutes; For 4 servings)

**Ingredients:**

- 4 (8 ounces) ribeye steaks
- 1 tablespoon McCormick Grill mates Montreal steak seasoning
- Salt
- Pepper

**Preparation:**

1. Insert the grill grate and close the hood
2. Pre-heat Ninja Foodi by pressing the "GRILL" option at and setting it to "HIGH" and timer to 10 minutes
3. Once it pre-heat until you hear a beep
4. Season the steak with steak seasoning and salt and pepper to taste
5. Cook for 4 minutes, open the hood and flip the steak
6. Cook for an additional 4 to 5 minutes
7. Remove the cooked steaks from the grill, then repeat steps for the remaining 2 steaks
8. Serve and enjoy!

**Nutritional Values Per Serving:**

Calories: 293 kcal, Carbs: 13 g, Fat: 22 g. Protein: 32 g

# Cumin-Paprika Rubbed Beef Brisket

(Prep time: 5 minutes; Cook time: 2 hours; For 12 servings)

**Ingredients:**

- 5 pounds brisket roast
- 5 tablespoons olive oil
- 1/4 teaspoon cayenne pepper
- 1 teaspoon garlic powder
- 1 teaspoon cumin, grounded
- 1 and 1/2 tablespoons paprika
- 1 teaspoon onion powder
- 2 teaspoons dry mustard

- 2 teaspoons black pepper, ground
- 2 teaspoons salt

**Preparation:**

1. Take a Ziploc bag and add all the ingredients into it

2. Marinate it in your fridge for at least 2 hours

3. Remove the grill grate from the unit

4. Pre-heat Ninja Foodi by pressing the "BAKE" option at 350 degrees F and timer to 30 minutes

5. Once it pre-heat until you hear a beep, then cook for 2 hours

6. Serve and enjoy!

**Nutritional Values Per Serving:**

Calories: 269 kcal, Carbs: 10 g, Fat: 13 g. Protein: 35 g

# Steak with Salsa Verde

(Prep time: 10 minutes; Cook time: 18 minutes; For 4 servings)

**Ingredients:**

- 2 beef flank steak, diced
- 2 cups salsa Verde
- 2 ripe avocados, diced
- 1 cup fresh cilantro leaves
- 2 medium tomatoes, seeded and diced
- 1/2 teaspoon salt
- 1/2 teaspoon pepper

**Preparation:**

1. Rub the steak with salt and pepper to season well

2. Pre-heat Ninja Foodi by pressing the "GRILL" option and setting it to "HIGH"

3. Once it pre-heat until you hear a beep, open the lid

4. Place the bread slices in the grill

5. Cover the lid and cook for 9 minutes

6. Flip it and cook for 9 minutes more

7. Blend salsa with cilantro in a blender, slice the steak and serve with salsa, tomato, and avocado

8. Serve and enjoy!

**Nutritional Values Per Serving:**

Calories: 545 kcal, Carbs: 15 g, Fat: 36.4 g. Protein: 42.5 g

# American Burger

(Prep time: 10 minutes; Cook time:20 minutes; For 4 servings)

**Ingredients:**

- 1 pound ground beef
- 4 seed hamburger buns, cut in half
- 1 tablespoon olive oil
- 1/2 cup bread crumbs
- 1 large egg, whisked
- 1/2 teaspoon salt
- 1/2 teaspoon pepper

**Preparation:**

1. Take all the ingredients for burger except oil and the bun in a bowl
2. Mix them and then make 4 of the ½ inch patties out of it
3. Brush these patties with olive oil
4. Pre-heat Ninja Foodi by pressing the "GRILL" option and setting it to "HIGH"
5. Once it pre-heat until you hear a beep, open the lid
6. Place 2 patties in the grill grate and cook for 5 minutes
7. Grill the remaining patties in the same way
8. Serve and enjoy!

**Nutritional Values Per Serving:**

Calories: 301 kcal, Carbs: 20 g, Fat: 15.8 g. Protein: 28.2 g

# Turkey Tomato Burgers

(Prep time: 5-10 minutes; Cook time: 40 minutes; For 6 servings)

**Ingredients:**

- 2 pounds lean turkey, grounded
- 6 burger buns of your choice, sliced in half
- 2/3 cup sun-dried tomatoes, chopped

- 1 cup feta cheese, crumbled
- 1/4 teaspoon salt
- 1/4 teaspoon pepper
- 1 large red onion, chopped

**Preparation:**

1. Take a mixing bowl, add all the ingredients and combine them well

2. Prepare six patties from the mixture

3. Arrange the grill grate and close the lid

4. Pre-heat Ninja Foodi by pressing the "GRILL" option and setting it to "MED" and timer to 14 minutes

5. Let it pre-heat until you hear a beep

6. Arrange the patties over the grill grate, lock lid and cook for 7 minutes more

7. Serve warm with ciabatta rolls and your favorite toppings

8. Enjoy!

**Nutritional Values Per Serving:**

Calories: 298 kcal, Carbs: 32 g, Fat: 16 g. Protein: 27.5 g

# Fantastic Coca-Cola Beef Roast

(Prep time: 10 minutes; Cook time:30-40 minutes; For 4 servings)

**Ingredients:**

- 2 pounds beef sirloin roast
- 2 garlic cloves, minced
- 1 can cola
- 1/2 cup of water
- 1 teaspoon salt
- 1 teaspoon pepper
- 1 bay leaf

**Preparation:**

1. Pre-heat Ninja Foodi by pressing the "ROAST" option and setting it to "400 Degrees F" and timer to 40 minutes

2. Let it pre-heat until you hear a beep

3. Arrange the listed ingredients in Grill Basket

4. Lock lid and cook until the timer goes to zero

5. Serve and enjoy!

**Nutritional Values Per Serving:**

Calories: 500 kcal, Carbs: 12 g, Fat: 21 g. Protein: 51 g

# Juicy Steak and Pineapple

(Prep time: 10 minutes; Cook time:8 minutes; For 4 servings)

**Ingredients:**

- 1/2 medium pineapple, cored and diced
- 1 jalapeno, seeded and stemmed, diced
- 1 medium red onion, diced
- 4 pieces filet mignon steaks, 6-8 ounces each
- 1 tablespoon canola oil
- Salt and pepper to taste
- 1 tablespoon lime juice
- 1/4 cup cilantro leaves, chopped
- Chili powder and ground coriander

**Preparation:**

1. Rub fillets with oil evenly, season them well with salt and pepper

2. Pre-heat Ninja Foodi by pressing the "GRILL" option and setting it to "HIGH" and timer to 8 minutes

3. Let it pre-heat until you hear a beep

4. Arrange fillets over grill grate, lock lid and cook for 4 minutes until the internal temperature reaches 125 degrees F

5. Take a mixing bowl and add pineapple, onion, jalapeno, mix well

6. Add lime juice, cilantro, chili powder, coriander and combine

7. Serve fillets with the pineapple mixture on top

8. Enjoy!

**Nutritional Values Per Serving:**

Calories: 530 kcal, Carbs: 21 g, Fat: 22 g. Protein: 58 g

# Onion and Beef Roast

(Prep time: 10 minutes; Cook time:30-40 minutes; For 4 servings)

**Ingredients:**

- 2 sticks celery, sliced
- 1 bulb garlic, peeled and crushed
- Bunch of herbs
- 2 pounds topside beef
- 2 medium onion, chopped
- Salt and pepper to taste
- 1 tablespoon butter
- 3 tablespoons olive oil

**Preparation:**

1.  Take a mixing bowl and add listed ingredients, combine well with each other

2.  Pre-heat Ninja Foodi by pressing the "ROAST" option and setting it to "380 Degrees F" and timer to 30 minutes

3.  Let it pre-heat until you hear a beep

4.  Arrange bowl mixture in your Nina Foodi Pan, cook until the timer reads zero

5.  Serve and enjoy!

**Nutritional Values Per Serving:**

Calories: 320 kcal, Carbs: 11 g, Fat: 17 g. Protein: 31 g

# Asian Pork Chops

(Prep time: 10 minutes; Cook time: 25 minutes; For 4 servings)

**Ingredients:**

- 1/4 cup hoisin sauce
- 1/4 cup hoisin sauce
- 1 teaspoon garlic powder
- 1 teaspoon onion powder
- 1/4 cup of soy sauce
- 1/4 cup apple cider vinegar
- 1 pound pork rib

**Preparation:**

1. Take a mixing bowl and add all listed ingredients, mix well

2. Add pork ribs and coat, let it chill for 2-4 hours

3. Pre-heat Ninja Foodi by pressing the "GRILL" option and setting it to "MED" and timer to 24 minutes

4. Let it pre-heat until you hear a beep

5. Arrange pork ribs over grill grate, lock lid and cook for 12 minutes, flip ribs and cook for 12 minutes more

6. Serve and enjoy!

**Nutritional Values Per Serving:**

Calories: 320 kcal, Carbs: 26 g, Fat: 9 g. Protein: 27 g

# Sweet Chipotle Ribs

(Prep time: 10 minutes; Cook time: 2 hours 5 minutes; For 6 servings)

**Ingredients:**

- 3 pounds baby back ribs
- 1 bottle(11.2-ounce beer)
- 1 tablespoon Dijon mustard
- 1 cup barbecue sauce
- Sauce
- 1/4 teaspoon pepper
- 1/8 cup Worcestershire sauce
- 1 tablespoon chipotle in adobo sauce, chopped
- 1/3 cup honey
- 2 teaspoons chipotle pepper, ground
- 1 and 1/2 cup ketchup
- 1/2 small onion, chopped
- 1/2 teaspoon salt
- 1/2 teaspoon garlic powder

**Preparation:**

1. Wrap the ribs in large foil and keep it aside

2. Pre-heat Ninja Foodi by pressing the "ROAST" option and setting it to "MED"

3. Once it pre-heat until you hear a beep, open the lid

4. Place the wrapped ribs slices in the grill grate

5. Cover the lid and cook for 1 hour and 30 minutes

6. Take a saucepan and rest of the ingredients and cook for 45 minutes on a simmer

7. Brush the grilled ribs with prepared sauce generously

8. Grill for 10 minutes more

9. Serve and enjoy!

**Nutritional Values Per Serving:**

Calories: 405 kcal, Carbs: 13 g, Fat: 23 g. Protein: 45 g

# Chapter 5: Healthy Vegetables and Side

## Grilled Sweet Potatoes

(Cook time: 16 minutes; For 4 servings)

**Ingredients:**

- 2 large sweet potatoes, sliced thinly
- ¼ tsp chipotle chili powder
- ½ tsp cumin
- ½ tsp paprika
- 1 tsp garlic powder
- 1 tsp chili powder
- 1 ½ tbsp olive oil

**Preparation:**

1.  Add sweet potato slices and remaining ingredients into the mixing bowl and toss well.
2.  Place the cooking pot in the unit then place the grill grate in the pot and close the hood.
3.  Select grill mode then set the temperature to medium and set the timer to 6 minutes. Press start to begin preheating.
4.  Once the unit is preheated it will beep then place sweet potato slices on grill grates and close the hood.
5.  Cook sweet potato slices for 3 minutes then flip sweet potato slices and continue cooking for 3 minutes.
6.  Serve and enjoy.

**Nutrition Values (Per Serving):**

Calories 79; Fat 5.5 g; Carbohydrates 7.7 g; Sugar 1.6 g; Protein 0.8 g; Cholesterol 0 mg

## Baked Lemon Broccoli

(Cook time: 35 minutes; For 4 servings)

**Ingredients:**

- 1 1/2 lbs broccoli florets
- 1/2 tsp garlic powder
- 2 1/2 tbsp olive oil

- 1 tbsp fresh lemon juice
- 1/4 tsp onion powder
- 1/4 tsp pepper
- 1/2 tsp salt

**Preparation:**

1. In a bowl, toss broccoli with onion powder, garlic powder, olive oil, pepper, and salt.

2. Place the cooking pot in the unit then close the hood.

3. Select bake mode then set the temperature to 390 F and set the timer to 25 minutes. Press start to begin preheating.

4. Once the unit is preheated it will beep then place broccoli florets in the cooking pot. Close the hood.

5. Cook broccoli for 25 minutes or until tender.

6. Drizzle lemon juice over broccoli and serve.

**Nutrition Values (Per Serving):**

Calories 134; Fat 9.3 g; Carbohydrates 11.8 g; Sugar 3 g; Protein 5 g; Cholesterol 0 mg

# Roasted Potatoes and Fancy Asparagus

(Prep time: 5-10 minutes; Cook time: 10 minutes; For 4 servings)

**Ingredients:**

- 1 pound asparagus, trimmed and sliced
- 4 potatoes, diced and boiled
- 1 teaspoon dill, dried
- 2 stalks scallions, chopped
- 1 tablespoon olive oil
- Salt and pepper, to taste

**Preparation:**

1. Take your asparagus and coat it with olive oil

2. Season well with scallions

3. Preheat your Ninja Foodi Smart XL Grill by pressing the "AIR CRISP" mode at 350 degrees F

4. Set the timer to 5 minutes

5. Transfer asparagus to the cooking basket

6. Cook for 5 minutes

7. Then transfer it to a bowl

8. Now, stir in remaining ingredients

9. Mix them well

10. Serve and enjoy!

## Nutritional Values Per Serving:

Calories: 222; Fat: 8 g; Saturated Fat: 3 g; Carbohydrates: 36 g; Fiber: 3 g; Sodium: 779 mg; Protein: 6 g

# Marinated Grilled Broccoli

(Cook time: 25 minutes; For 6 servings)

## Ingredients:

- 4 cups broccoli florets
- 1 ½ tsp garlic, minced
- 1 ½ tsp Italian seasoning
- 1 tbsp lemon juice
- 4 tbsp olive oil
- ¼ tsp pepper
- 1 ¼ tsp kosher salt

## Preparation:

1. Add broccoli and remaining ingredients into the mixing bowl and mix well. Cover and place in the refrigerator for 2 hours.

2. Place the cooking pot in the unit then place the grill grate in the pot and close the hood.

3. Select grill mode then set the temperature to medium and set the timer to 6 minutes. Press start to begin preheating.

4. Once the unit is preheated it will beep then place marinated broccoli florets on grill grates and close the hood.

5. Cook broccoli for 3 minutes then flip broccoli and continue cooking for 3 minutes.

6. Serve and enjoy.

## Nutritional Values Per Serving:

Calories 106; Fat 9.9 g; Carbohydrates 4.5 g; Sugar 1.2 g; Protein 1.8 g; Cholesterol 1 mg

# Healthy Root Vegetables

(Cook time: 40 minutes; For 4 servings)

**Ingredients:**

- 1 parsnip, cut into 1-inch chunks
- 3 medium carrots, cut into 1-inch pieces
- 2 tsp Italian seasoning
- 1 onion, cut into wedges
- 1 rutabaga, peeled and cut into 1-inch chunks
- 1 tbsp olive oil
- 2 tbsp vinegar
- Pepper
- Salt

**Preparation:**

1. In a bowl, toss vegetables with remaining ingredients.

2. Place the cooking pot in the unit then close the hood.

3. Select bake mode then set the temperature to 390 F and set the timer to 30 minutes. Press start to begin preheating.

4. Once the unit is preheated it will beep then place vegetables in the cooking pot. Close the hood.

5. Cook vegetables for 25-30 minutes.

6. Serve and enjoy.

**Nutrition Values (Per Serving):**

Calories 125; Fat 4.5 g; Carbohydrates 20 g; Sugar 10.7 g; Protein 2.3 g; Cholesterol 2 mg

# Cheesy Cauliflower Florets

(Cook time: 40 minutes; For 6 servings)

**Ingredients:**

- 1 medium cauliflower head, cut into florets
- 1 tsp garlic, minced
- 1/2 cup butter, melted
- 1/2 cup parmesan cheese, grated

- 1 cup breadcrumbs
- 1/4 tsp pepper
- 1/4 tsp salt

**Preparation:**

1. In a small bowl, mix melted butter and garlic.

2. In a shallow dish, mix parmesan cheese, breadcrumbs, pepper, and salt.

3. Dip each cauliflower floret into the melted butter and coat with parmesan cheese mixture.

4. Place the cooking pot in the unit then close the hood.

5. Select bake mode then set the temperature to 400 F and set the timer to 30 minutes. Press start to begin preheating.

6. Once the unit is preheated it will beep then place coated cauliflower florets in the cooking pot. Close the hood.

7. Cook cauliflower florets for 30 minutes.

8. Serve and enjoy.

**Nutritional Values Per Serving:** Calories 281; Fat 19 g; Carbohydrates 18 g; Sugar 3.4 g; Protein 9.8 g; Cholesterol 51 mg

# Baked Broccoli Cauliflower

(Cook time: 30 minutes; For 6 servings)

**Ingredients:**

- 4 cups cauliflower florets
- 4 cups broccoli florets
- 2/3 cup parmesan cheese, shredded
- 4 garlic cloves, minced
- 1/3 cup olive oil
- Pepper
- Salt

**Preparation:**

1. Add half parmesan cheese, broccoli, cauliflower, garlic, oil, pepper, and salt into the large bowl and toss well.

2. Place the cooking pot in the unit then close the hood.

3.  Select bake mode then set the temperature to 390 F and set the timer to 20 minutes. Press start to begin preheating.

4.  Once the unit is preheated it will beep then place cauliflower broccoli mixture in the cooking pot. Close the hood.

5.  Cook for 20 minutes.

6.  Add remaining cheese.

7.  Toss well and serve.

**Nutrition Values (Per Serving):**

Calories 165; Fat 13.6 g; Carbohydrates 8.6 g; Sugar 3 g; Protein 6.4 g; Cholesterol 7 mg

# Lemon Pepper Brussels Sprouts

(Prep time: 5-10 minutes; Cook time: 10 minutes; For 4 servings)

**Ingredients:**

*   1 pound brussels sprouts, sliced
*   2 teaspoons lemon pepper seasoning
*   2 tablespoons olive oil
*   Salt, to taste

**Preparation:**

1.  Take your Brussels and coat it with olive oil

2.  Season your sprouts with lemon pepper and salt

3.  Spread the prepared Brussels over the Cooking basket

4.  Preheat your Ninja Foodi Smart XL Grill by pressing the "BAKE" mode at 350 degrees F

5.  Set the timer to 5 minutes

6.  Cook for 5 minutes

7.  Serve and enjoy!

**Nutritional Values Per Serving:**

Calories: 229; Fat: 18 g; Saturated Fat: 2 g; Carbohydrates: 12 g; Fiber: 2 g; Sodium: 360 mg; Protein: 8 g

# Balsamic Tomatoes Roast

(Prep time: 5-10 minutes; Cook time: 5 minutes; For 4 servings)

**Ingredients:**

- 1 pound tomatoes, sliced into quarters
- ½ cup balsamic vinegar
- 1 teaspoon Italian seasoning

**Preparation:**

1. Take your tomatoes and toss them well in vinegar
2. Season them with Italian seasoning
3. Transfer to Air Crisping basket
4. Preheat your Ninja Foodi Smart XL Grill by pressing the "AIR CRISP" at 350 degrees F
5. Set the timer for 5 minutes
6. Transfer them to the cooking basket
7. Cook for 5 minutes or more if needed
8. Serve and enjoy!

**Nutritional Values Per Serving:**

Calories: 174; Fat: 14 g; Saturated Fat: 3 g; Carbohydrates: 12 g; Fiber: 2 g; Sodium: 11 mg; Protein: 2 g

# Cheesy Brussels sprouts

(Cook time: 35 minutes; For 4 servings)

**Ingredients:**

- 15 oz Brussels sprouts, trimmed and cut in half
- 3 garlic cloves, minced
- 3 tbsp olive oil
- 1/4 cup breadcrumbs
- 1/4 cup parmesan cheese, grated
- Pepper
- Salt

**Preparation:**

1. In a mixing bowl, toss Brussels sprouts with breadcrumbs, cheese, garlic, oil, pepper, and salt until well coated.

2. Place the cooking pot in the unit then close the hood.

3. Select bake mode then set the temperature to 390 F and set the timer to 25 minutes. Press start to begin preheating.

4. Once the unit is preheated it will beep then place Brussels sprouts in the cooking pot. Close the hood.

5. Cook Brussels sprouts for 25 minutes.

6. Serve and enjoy.

**Nutrition Values (Per Serving):**

Calories 206; Fat 13.7 g; Carbohydrates 16.3 g; Sugar 3 g; Protein 8.5 g; Cholesterol 8 mg

# Cinnamon Roasted Butternut Squash

(Cook time: 50 minutes; For 4 servings)

**Ingredients:**

- 3 lbs butternut squash, peeled, seeded, and cut into 1-inch cubes
- 1 1/2 tbsp olive oil
- 1/2 tsp cinnamon
- 1 1/2 tbsp maple syrup
- Pepper
- Salt

**Preparation:**

1. In a mixing bowl, toss squash cubes with remaining ingredients.

2. Place the cooking pot in the unit then close the hood.

3. Select bake mode then set the temperature to 400 F and set the timer to 40 minutes. Press start to begin preheating.

4. Once the unit is preheated it will beep then place squash in the cooking pot. Close the hood.

5. Cook squash cubes for 35-40 minutes.

6. Serve and enjoy.

**Nutrition Values (Per Serving):**

Calories 220; Fat 5.6 g; Carbohydrates 45 g; Sugar 12 g; Protein 3.4 g; Cholesterol 0 mg

# Perfect Grill Cauliflower Steaks

(Cook time: 20 minutes; For 4 servings)

**Ingredients:**

- 1 medium cauliflower head, cut into ½-inch thick slices

- ½ cup parmesan cheese, grated
- ½ tsp onion powder
- ½ tsp chili powder
- ½ tsp lemon pepper seasoning
- ½ tsp dried thyme
- 2 tbsp soy sauce
- 4 garlic cloves, minced
- ¼ cup olive oil
- Pepper
- Salt

## Preparation:

1. In a small bowl, mix onion powder, chili powder, lemon pepper seasoning, thyme, soy sauce, garlic, olive oil, pepper, and salt.
2. Brush cauliflower slices with spice and oil mixture.
3. Place the cooking pot in the unit then place grill grate in the pot and close the hood.
4. Select grill mode then set the temperature to medium and set the timer to 5 minutes. Press start to begin preheating.
5. Once the unit is preheated it will beep then place cauliflower slices on grill grates and close the hood.
6. Cook cauliflower slices for 5 minutes then flip cauliflower slices and continue cooking for 5 minutes.
7. Sprinkle with grated parmesan cheese and serve.

## Nutrition Values (Per Serving):

Calories 157; Fat 12.9 g; Carbohydrates 10 g; Sugar 3.8 g; Protein 3.7 g; Cholesterol 0 mg

# Juicy Garlic Carrots

(Prep time: 5-10 minutes; Cook time: 10 minutes; For 4 servings)

## Ingredients:

- 1 pound carrots, diced
- 2 teaspoons garlic powder
- 2 tablespoons olive oil
- Salt and pepper, to taste

## Preparation:

1.  Add carrot cubes in a bowl

2.  Toss them with oil

3.  Season the cube further with garlic pepper, salt, and pepper

4.  Coat them equally

5.  Spread the carrots in the Air Crisp basket

9.  Preheat your Ninja Foodi Smart XL Grill by pressing the "AIR CRISP" mode at 390 degrees F

6.  Set the timer for 30 minutes

7.  Stir it after every 10 minutes

8.  Once cooked, serve immediately

9.  Enjoy!

**Nutritional Values Per Serving:**

Calories: 183; Fat: 11 g; Saturated Fat: 5 g; Carbohydrates: 21 g; Fiber: 1 g; Sodium: 440 mg; Protein: 2 g

# Baked Broccoli & Brussels

(Cook time: 40 minutes; For 6 servings)

## Ingredients:

*   1 lb Brussels sprouts, cut ends

*   1 lb broccoli, cut into florets

*   1 tsp garlic powder

*   1/2 tsp pepper

*   3 tbsp olive oil

*   1/2 onion, chopped

*   1 tsp paprika

*   3/4 tsp salt

## Preparation:

1.  Add all ingredients into the mixing bowl and toss well.

2.  Place the cooking pot in the unit then close the hood.

3.  Select bake mode then set the temperature to 390 F and set the timer to 30 minutes. Press start to begin preheating.

4.  Once the unit is preheated it will beep then place the veggie mixture in the cooking pot. Close the hood.

5. Cook vegetables for 30 minutes.

6. Serve and enjoy.

**Nutrition Values (Per Serving):**

Calories 126; Fat 7.6 g; Carbohydrates 14 g; Sugar 3.5 g; Protein 5 g; Cholesterol 0 mg

# Spicy Chickpeas

(Prep time: 5-10 minutes; Cook time: 10 minutes; For 4 servings)

**Ingredients:**

- 15 ounces chickpeas, canned, rinsed, and drained
- 1 tablespoon olive oil
- 1 teaspoon cumin, grounded
- 1 teaspoon chili powder
- ½ teaspoon cayenne pepper
- Salt, to taste

**Preparation:**

1. Take your chickpeas and coat it with olive oil

2. Add cayenne, chili powder, cumin, pepper, and salt into a mixing bowl

3. Season them well

4. Transfer them to a crisp tray

5. Preheat your Ninja Foodi Smart XL Grill by pressing the "AIR CRISP" mode at 390 degrees F

6. Set the timer to 10 minutes

7. Cook and stir occasionally

8. Serve and enjoy!

**Nutritional Values Per Serving:**

Calories: 182; Fat: 7 g; Saturated Fat: 3 g; Carbohydrates: 25 g; Fiber: 4 g; Sodium: 264 mg; Protein: 0 g

# Chapter 6: Surprise Snacks and Appetizers

## Chocolate Marshmallow Banana

(Prep time: 10 minutes; Cook time: 5 minutes; For 2 servings)

**Ingredients:**

- 2 bananas, peeled
- 1 cup chocolate chips
- 1 cup mini marshmallows

**Preparation:**

1.  Select the "Grill" button on the Ninja Foodi Smart XL Grill and regulate the settings at Medium for 5 minutes.

2.  Arrange the banana on a foil paper and cut it lengthwise, leaving behind the ends.

3.  Insert the chocolate chips and marshmallows in the bananas and tightly wrap the foil.

4.  Arrange the filled bananas inside the Ninja Foodi when it displays "Add Food".

5.  Dole out in a platter and unwrap to serve and enjoy.

**Nutritional Values Per Serving:**

Calories: 137; Fat: 1g; Sat Fat: 0.6g; Carbohydrates: 33.3g

## Grilled Donut Ice Cream Sandwich

(Prep time: 10 minutes; Cook time: 3 minutes; For 4 servings)

**Ingredients:**

- 4 glazed donuts, cut in half
- 8 scoops vanilla ice cream
- 1 cup cream, whipped
- 4 cherries, maraschino

**Preparation:**

1.  Select the "Grill" button on the Ninja Foodi Smart XL Grill and regulate the settings at Medium for 3 minutes.

2.  Arrange the donut halves, glazed side down in the Ninja Foodi when it displays "Add Food".

3.  Dole out in a platter and stuff vanilla ice cream inside each donut sandwich.

4. Top with whipped cream and cherry to serve.

**Nutritional Values Per Serving:**

Calories: 558; Fat: 27.5g; Sat Fat: 13.2g; Carbohydrates: 70.9g; Fiber: 2.5g; Sugar: 28.4g

# Flavorful Taco Cups

(Prep time: 5-10 minutes; Cook time: 10 minutes; For 4 servings)

**Ingredients:**

- 1 cup cheddar cheese, shredded
- 2 tablespoons taco seasoning
- ½ cup tomatoes, chopped
- 1 pound ground beef, cooked
- 12 wonton wrappers

**Preparation:**

1. Press wrappers firmly onto the muffin pan
2. Transfer the pan inside your Ninja Foodi Smart XL
3. Air Fry on AIR CRISP mode for 5 minutes at 400 degrees F
4. Top with ground beef and tomatoes,
5. Sprinkle taco seasoning, cheese
6. Air Fry for 5 minutes more
7. Enjoy!

**Nutritional Values Per Serving:**

Calories: 431; Fat: 21 g; Saturated Fat: 7 g; Carbohydrates: 30 g; Fiber: 5 g; Sodium: 604 mg; Protein: 31 g

# Cream Crepes

(Prep time: 10 minutes; Cook time: 16 minutes; For 6 servings)

**Ingredients:**

- 3 organic eggs
- 1½ teaspoons Splenda
- 3 tablespoons coconut flour
- 3 tablespoons coconut oil, melted and divided

- ½ cup heavy cream

**Preparation:**

1. Select the "Grill" button on the Ninja Foodi Smart XL Grill and regulate the settings at Medium for 12 minutes.

2. Mingle together 1½ tablespoons of coconut oil, Splenda, eggs and salt in a bowl.

3. Slowly fold in the coconut flour and heavy cream.

4. Pour about ¼ of the mixture inside the Ninja Foodi when it displays "Add Food".

5. Grill for 5 minutes, flipping once in between.

6. Repeat with the remaining mixture in batches and serve.

**Nutritional Values Per Serving:**

Calories: 145; Fat: 13.1g; Sat Fat: 9.1g; Carbohydrates: 4g; Fiber: 1.5g; Sugar: 1.2g; Protein: 3.5g

# Stuffed Up Chicken with Herbs and Cream

(Prep time: 5-10 minutes; Cook time: 15 minutes; For 4 servings)

**Ingredients:**

- 4 ounces garlic and herb cream cheese
- Salt and pepper to taste
- 2 teaspoons dried Italian seasoning
- Olive oil as needed
- 2 chicken breast fillets

**Preparation:**

1. Take the chicken and brush them with oil

2. Season them with salt, pepper, and Italian seasoning

3. Top them with garlic and herb cream cheese

4. Roll up the chicken carefully

5. Transfer them to the Air Crisping basket

6. Place the basket inside the appliance

7. AIR FRY for 7 minutes per side, at 370 degrees F

8. Serve and enjoy!

**Nutritional Values Per Serving:**

Calories: 750; Fat: 42 g; Saturated Fat: 10 g; Carbohydrates: 18 g; Fiber: 3 g; Sodium: 846 mg; Protein: 73 g

# Blooming Grilled Apples

(Prep time: 10 minutes; Cook time: 30 minutes; For 4 servings)

**Ingredients:**

- 8 tablespoons maple cream caramel sauce, divided
- 4 small baking apples
- 12 teaspoons chopped pecans, divided

**Preparation:**

1. Select the "Grill" button on the Ninja Foodi Smart XL Grill and regulate the settings for 30 minutes.

2. Trim the upper part of the apples and scoop out the cores of the apples.

3. Chop the apple around the center and insert fine cuts surrounding the apple.

4. Shove the pecans and maple cream caramel sauce in the middle of the apple.

5. Cover the apple with the foil and arrange the apple inside the Ninja Foodi when it displays "Add Food".

6. Dole out in a platter and to serve immediately.

**Nutritional Values Per Serving:**

Calories: 407; Fat: 23g; Sat Fat: 12g; Carbohydrates: 50g; Fiber: 50g; Sugar: 32.4g; Protein: 4g

# Meaty Bratwursts

(Prep time: 5-10 minutes; Cook time: 12 minutes; For 6 servings)

**Ingredients:**

- 1 pack bratwursts

**Preparation:**

1. Preheat your Ninja Foodi Smart XL in AIR CRISP mode for 5 minutes at 350 degrees F

2. Add bratwurst to the Cooking basket

3. Cook for 10 minutes, making sure to flip once

4. Enjoy!

**Nutritional Values Per Serving:**

Calories: 739; Fat: 57 g; Saturated Fat: 20 g; Carbohydrates: 13 g; Fiber: 3 g; Sodium: 2641 mg; Protein: 37 g

# Simple Garlic Bread

(Prep time: 5-10 minutes; Cook time: 5 minutes; For 4 servings)

**Ingredients:**

- Salt to taste
- 1 Italian loaf of bread
- 1 tablespoon fresh parsley, chopped
- ½ cup butter, melted
- 4 garlic cloves, chopped

**Preparation:**

1. Take a bowl and add parsley, butter, and garlic
2. Spread the mixture on the bread slices
3. Transfer the bread inside the Ninja Foodi Smart XL cooking basket
4. Cook at 400 degrees F for 3 minutes on AIR CRISP mode
5. Serve and enjoy once done

**Nutritional Values Per Serving:**

Calories: 155; Fat: 7 g; Saturated Fat: 2 g; Carbohydrates: 20 g; Fiber: 3 g; Sodium: 227 mg; Protein: 28 g

# Grilled Fruit Skewers

(Prep time: 20 minutes; Cook time: 12 minutes; For 12 servings)

**Ingredients:**

- 8 peaches, sliced
- 1½ pints strawberries, sliced
- 1½ cups pineapples, cut into large cubes
- 3 tablespoons honey
- Salt, to taste
- 3 tablespoons olive oil
- 10 skewers, soaked in water for 20 minutes

**Preparation:**

1. Select the "Grill" button on the Ninja Foodi Smart XL Grill and regulate the settings at Medium for 12 minutes.

2. Insert the strawberries, pineapples, and peaches on the skewers.

3. Dust with salt and shower with olive oil.

4. Arrange the skewers inside the Ninja Foodi when it displays "Add Food".

5. Grill for 12 minutes, turning twice in between.

6. Trickle the grilled fruits with honey and serve well.

**Nutritional Values Per Serving:**

Calories: 132; Fat: 4.7g; Sat Fat: 0.6g; Carbohydrates: 23.8g

# Cute Mozarella Bites

(Prep time: 5-10 minutes; Cook time: 8 minutes; For 12 servings)

**Ingredients:**

- 1 cup breadcrumbs

- ¼ cup butter, melted

- 12 mozzarella strips

**Preparation:**

1. Dip the mozzarella strips in butter

2. Dredge them with breadcrumbs

3. Add mozzarella strips to your Ninja Foodi Smart XL Crisping basket

4. Cook at 320 degrees F for 8 minutes on AIR CRISP mode

5. Cook for 8 minutes, making sure to flip once

6. Serve and enjoy!

**Nutritional Values Per Serving:**

Calories: 206; Fat: 12 g; Saturated Fat: 5 g; Carbohydrates: 16 g; Fiber: 5 g; Sodium: 284 mg; Protein: 10 g

# S'mores Roll-Up

(Prep time: 10 minutes; Cook time: 5 minutes; For 2 servings)

**Ingredients:**

- 4 graham crackers

- 2 cups mini marshmallows

- 2 flour tortillas

- 2 cups chocolate chips

## Preparation:

1. Select the "Grill" button on the Ninja Foodi Smart XL Grill and regulate the settings at Medium for 5 minutes.

2. Split the graham crackers, chocolate chips, and marshmallows on the tortillas.

3. Tightly wrap up the tortillas and arrange them inside the Ninja Foodi when it displays "Add Food".

4. Grill for 5 minutes, flipping once in between.

5. Dole out in a plate when completely grilled to serve.

## Nutritional Values Per Serving:

Calories: 429; Fat: 13.6g; Sat Fat: 6g; Carbohydrates: 72.7g; Fiber: 3.3g; Sugar: 57.8g; Protein: 5.9g

# Original Crispy Tomatoes

(Prep time: 5-10 minutes; Cook time: 5 minutes; For 4 servings)

## Ingredients:

- Bread crumbs as needed
- ½ cup buttermilk
- ¼ cup almond flour
- Salt and pepper to taste
- ¼ tablespoon Creole seasoning
- 1 green tomato

## Preparation:

1. Preheat Ninja Foodi Smart XL by pressing the "AIR CRISP" option and setting it to "400 Degrees F" and timer to 5 minutes

2. let it preheat until you hear a beep

3. Add flour to your plate and take another plate and add buttermilk

4. Cut tomatoes and season with salt and pepper

5. Make a mix of creole seasoning and crumbs

6. Take tomato slice and cover with flour, place in buttermilk and then into crumbs

7. Repeat with all tomatoes

8. Cook the tomato slices for 5 minutes

9. Serve with basil and enjoy!

## Nutritional Values Per Serving:

Calories: 200; Fat: 12 g; Saturated Fat: 4 g; Carbohydrates: 11 g; Fiber: 2 g; Sodium: 1203 mg; Protein: 3 g

# Hearty Sausage Patties

(Prep time: 5-10 minutes; Cook time: 10 minutes; For 2 servings)

**Ingredients:**

- 1 pack sausage patties

**Preparation:**

1. Transfer sausages to the Air Fryer cooking basket
2. Select the Air Crisp Mode and set the temperature to 400 degrees F
3. Cook for 5 minutes per side
4. Serve and enjoy once done!

**Nutritional Values Per Serving:**

Calories: 228; Fat: 13 g; Saturated Fat: 5 g; Carbohydrates: 5 g; Fiber: 2 g; Sodium: 145 mg; Protein: 21 g

# Mustard Veggie Mix

(Prep time: 5-10 minutes; Cook time: 30-40 minutes; For 4 servings)

**Ingredients:**

**Vinaigrette**

- ½ cup olive oil
- ½ cup avocado oil
- ¼ teaspoon pepper
- 1 teaspoon salt
- 2 tablespoons honey
- ½ cup red wine vinegar
- 2 tablespoons Dijon vinegar

**Veggies**

- 4 zucchinis, halved
- 4 sweet onion, quartered
- 4 red pepper, seeded and halved
- 2 bunch green onions, trimmed
- 4 yellow squash, cut in half

**Preparation:**

1. Take a small bowl and whisk in mustard, honey, vinegar, salt, and pepper. Add oil and mix well

2. Set your Ninja Foodi Smart XL to GRILL mode and MED setting, set timer to 10 minutes

3. Transfer onion quarter to Grill Grate, cook for 5 minutes

4. Flip and cook for 5 minutes more

5. Grill remaining veggies in the same way, giving 7 minutes per side for zucchini and 1 minute for green onions

6. Serve with mustard vinaigrette on top

7. Enjoy!

**Nutritional Values Per Serving:**

Calories: 327; Fat: 5 g; Saturated Fat: 0.5 g; Carbohydrates:328 g; Fiber: 2 g; Sodium: 524 mg; Protein: 8 g

# Chocolate Peanut Butter Cups

(Prep time: 10 minutes; Cook time: 30 minutes; For 4 servings)

**Ingredients:**

- ¼ cup heavy cream
- 1 cup butter
- 2 ounces unsweetened chocolate
- 4 packets stevia
- ¼ cup peanut butter, separated

**Preparation:**

1. Select the "Bake" button on the Ninja Foodi Smart XL Grill and regulate the settings at 360 degrees F for 30 minutes.

2. Microwave the peanut butter and butter for 1 minute in a bowl.

3. Mingle in the unsweetened chocolate, stevia, and heavy cream.

4. Pour the peanut butter mixture in a baking mold.

5. Arrange the baking mold inside the Ninja Foodi when it displays "Add Food".

6. Bake for 30 minutes, turning twice in between.

7. Trickle the grilled fruits with honey and serve

**Nutritional Values Per Serving:**

Calories: 479; Fat: 51.5g; Sat Fat: 29.7g; Carbohydrates: 7.7g; Fiber: 2.7g; Sugar: 1.4g; Protein: 5.2g

# Fancy Lush Baked Apples

(Prep time: 5-10 minutes; Cook time: 10 minutes; For 4 servings)

**Ingredients:**

- 1 teaspoon cinnamon
- Zest of 1 orange
- 1 and ½ ounces mixed seeds
- 1 and ¾ ounces fresh breadcrumbs
- 2 tablespoons brown sugar
- ¾ ounces butter
- 4 apples

**Preparation:**

1. Preheat Ninja Foodi Smart XL by pressing the "AIR CRISP" option and setting it to "356 Degrees F" and timer to 10 minutes

2. Prepare apples by scoring skin around the circumference and coring them using a knife

3. Take cored apples and stuff the listed ingredients

4. Transfer apples to Air Fryer basket and bake for 10 minutes

5. Serve and enjoy!

**Nutritional Values Per Serving:**

Calories: 150; Fat: 5 g; Saturated Fat: 1 g; Carbohydrates: 35 g; Fiber: 3 g; Sodium: 10 mg; Protein: 1 g

# Fudge Divine

(Prep time: 20 minutes; Cook time: 14 minutes; For 8 servings)

**Ingredients:**

- 1 cup heavy whipping cream
- ½ teaspoon organic vanilla extract
- 2-ounce butter, softened
- 2-ounce 70% dark chocolate, finely chopped

**Preparation:**

1. Select the "Bake" button on the Ninja Foodi Smart XL Grill and regulate the settings at 360 degrees F for 14 minutes.

2. Mingle cream with vanilla, butter, and chocolate in a bowl.

3. Pour the cream mixture in a baking mold.

4. Arrange the baking mold inside the Ninja Foodi when it displays "Add Food".

5. Bake for 14 minutes and dole out in a dish.

6. Refrigerate it for few hours and serve chilled.

**Nutritional Values Per Serving:**

Calories: 292; Fat: 26.2g; Sat Fat: 16.3g; Carbohydrates: 8.2g; Fiber: 0g; Sugar: 6.6g; Protein: 5.2g

# Well-Seasoned Garlic Carrots

(Prep time: 5-10 minutes; Cook time: 10 minutes; For 4 servings)

**Ingredients:**

- Salt and pepper to taste
- 2 teaspoons garlic powder
- 2 tablespoons olive oil
- 1 pound carrots, diced

**Preparation:**

1. Take a bowl and toss the carrot cubes generously in oil

2. Season the cube further with salt, pepper, and garlic powder

3. Make sure that they are coated evenly

4. Spread the carrots in the Air Crisp Basket

5. Set your Ninja Foodi Smart XL to 390 degrees F in AIR CRISP mode and set the timer to 30 minutes

6. Cook for 10 minutes, making sure to stir once

7. Serve and enjoy!

**Nutritional Values Per Serving:**

Calories: 183; Fat: 11 g; Saturated Fat: 5 g; Carbohydrates: 21 g; Fiber: 1 g; Sodium: 440 mg; Protein: 2 g

# Grilled Pineapple Sundaes

(Prep time: 10 minutes; Cook time: 4 minutes; For 4 servings)

**Ingredients:**

- 2 tablespoons sweetened coconut, toasted and shredded
- 4 scoops vanilla ice cream
- 4 pineapple slices
- Dulce de leche, for drizzling

**Preparation:**

1. Select the "Grill" button on the Ninja Foodi Smart XL Grill and regulate the settings at Medium for 4 minutes.

2. Arrange the pineapple slices in the Ninja Foodi when it displays "Add Food".

3. Grill for about 4 minutes, turning once in between.

4. Dole out in a plate when completely grilled.

5. Place the scoops of vanilla ice cream over the grilled pineapple slices.

6. Trickle Dulce de leche and shredded coconut over the pineapples to serve.

**Nutritional Values Per Serving:**

Calories: 338; Fat: 9.5g; Sat Fat: 6.3g; Carbohydrates: 61g; Fiber: 3g; Sugar: 46.2g; Protein: 5.3g

CPSIA information can be obtained
at www.ICGtesting.com
Printed in the USA
LVHW102308020321
680445LV00010B/153